THE GIFT OF CHARITY

Wrapped in a Korowai of Love

THE GIFT OF CHARITY

Wrapped in a Korowai of Love

Kerry Owen with Lisa Knowlton

CFI
An imprint of Cedar Fort, Inc.
Springville, Utah

Paperback ISBN 13: 978-1-4621-4999-5
eBook ISBN 13: 978-1-4621-5000-7

Published by CFI, an imprint of Cedar Fort, Inc.
2373 W. 700 S., Suite 100, Springville, UT 84663
Distributed by Cedar Fort, Inc., www.cedarfort.com

Library of Congress Cataloging Number: 2025942644

Cover design by Shawnda Craig

Edited by Emily Clark
Typeset by Liz Kazandzhy

Printed in the United States of America

10 9 8 7 6 5 4 3 2 1

Printed on acid-free paper

From Kerry:

To my parents, who taught me faith, hard work, and compassion.

To my in-laws, who raised a good man and welcomed me with love.

To my husband and children—your support has sustained me, and your sacrifices are woven into every page.

To those who stood by me—who served alongside me, helped my family, believed in my dreams, and offered strength in both quiet and extraordinary ways.

To the teachers who trusted me.

To the mentors who shaped me.

To those who helped bring this book to life.

And to the children and youth I saw in my dreams—this book is for you.

May it find you and remind you of your worth, your voice, and your purpose.

From Lisa:

To Ben, who has always believed in me and helped me find my wings.

Contents

Prologue: The Queen's Signature 1
1 Korowai 3
2 Awareness of Suffering and Injustice 6
3 Experience with Suffering, Injustice, and Comfort 9
4 Marriage, Children, and My Inner Voice 12
5 Embracing a New Land and a New Culture 15
6 Learning to Follow My Inner Voice 17
7 The First Dream 21
8 Second Dream 25
9 Third Dream 29
10 An Extraordinary Conversation 31
11 Adopting 183 Children 34
12 Miracles 37
13 Charity Work Is All About *Love* *41*
14 Are You Two Sisters? 45
15 Can I Quit? 48

16 Meaningful Connections 51
17 Unseen Help 56
18 Immeasurable Donations. 59
19 More Compassion, Less Judgement 63
20 Hope. 66
21 Facing Opposition. 71
22 A Challenge to Prove That God Is Real. 77
23 Eyes That See 80
24 Anxious to Do More Good 85
25 God Knows Us by Name 90
26 My Epiphany 93
27 Serving the One 97
About the Author 103

Prologue

The Queen's Signature

ELIZABETH THE SECOND, by the Grace of God Queen of New Zealand and Her Other Realms and Territories, Head of the Commonwealth, Defender of the Faith & Sovereign of The New Zealand Order of Merit, to Our trusty and well beloved KERRY LOUISE OWEN.

I FIND MYSELF ONCE AGAIN DRAWN TO THE CERTIFICATE THAT MY husband framed for me, now hanging on the wall of our home. There is my name. Not *just* "Kerry Owen", but "*trusty and well beloved*" Kerry Louise Owen. Queen Elizabeth the Second had *touched* this same certificate and *written* her signature. Never had I imagined, even in my childhood daydreams, that I would one day receive an honour from the Queen.

Like most girls growing up in England, I loved Princess Diana. I was naturally reserved like she was, blushed easily, and was blonde.

So, of course, I had convinced myself that I looked just like her. I had even persuaded a neighbour boy to dress up like Prince Charles so we could reenact their Royal Wedding. To me, British royalty had always been associated with palaces, crowns, and all the trappings portrayed in British period dramas. Any royal correspondence was sealed with elaborate red wax and delivered on a silver tray by a white-gloved, uniformed servant. All fictional, imaginary, right?

Yet, here was evidence to the contrary on my wall right in front of me. I had received a Royal Honour from the Queen—minus the red sealing wax, silver tray, and white-gloved servant!

I think about everything that this honour stands for. The journey here was far from a fairytale. It all started with children: the children I saw in my dreams, their faces hungry and yearning. I think about the decade-long struggle to make my dreams come true. I think about the time when I had literally gotten up out of my hospital bed to deliver my first speech on camera. I think about the resistance, criticism, and roadblocks along the way that often left me feeling inadequate and questioning my resolve to keep going. I think about my family and the sacrifices we *all* made.

This framed certificate of honour has *my* name written on it, yet I see in its reflection the hundreds of faces of those people who worked alongside me, making this all possible—faces of many colours and cultures. I also see the faces of those children from my dreams, now full of hope and smiling back at me through the glass covering the Queen's signature—faces that will be forever etched in my heart and mind.

Perhaps dreams are not just dreams. Perhaps the most rewarding journeys are hard. Perhaps true tales are better than fairy tales.

Chapter 1

Korowai

The soft weight of the Korowai, a traditional Māori cloak made of iridescent feathers, settled upon me like an embrace as Marion placed it around my shoulders. As I looked at the beautiful blue and green feathers cascading down the length of this ceremonial cloak, an unexpected and powerful feeling of love and support came over me.

Marion, the grandmother of my adopted daughter, smiled at me. "This cloak represents the arms of love, comfort, and support of family—past, present, and future." I hadn't expected to feel the embrace of those arms in the form of this cloak but it was ever present in the light caress of feathers all around me. *After all, I am not Māori,* I thought. *This is not my biological family, and these are not my ancestors.* Yet, despite these facts, this feeling of love was undeniable. I stood still, soaking it all in, and I could not keep myself from crying.

As Marion continued to tie the Korowai in place with black tassels about my neck, I saw that she too had tears welling up in her green eyes as they locked on mine. Despite our differences, she considered me family, and I was humbled that she thought me worthy of such an honour on this day of honours.

Along with other Royal Honour recipients, I was led to two large, walnut-coloured wooden doors. As we stood in line, a wave of familiarity washed over me. *I have been here before,* I thought—*not physically, but . . .*

Almost a decade earlier, I had seen myself here in a dream, in this very same building, standing at these very same wooden doors. A Māori man, holding a ring of keys, motioned for me to go through the doors. As I did so, I walked into a brilliant bright light. That is where my dream ended. Ever since, I had always questioned what was beyond those doors? Where was the light coming from? Why did it shine so brightly? To be physically now where that dream had put me years before was surreal. I was eager to finally discover the source of that light. On this day, however, I discovered there was no brilliant, bright light—only silence. From the silence came a powerful female voice that rang out with a soul-stirring Māori call, welcoming us into the ceremony. "Haere mai . . . haere mai ra," she projected, causing a reverent hush to fall over the crowd. This was our cue to start walking down the red carpet.

My heart thumped in my chest as I entered the great hall. The space was majestic, with sparkling chandeliers, brocade drapery, and a rich wooden floor divided by a red carpet. Members of the audience, sitting on both sides of the carpet, watched our procession enter with an air of esteem.

My gaze was immediately drawn to an imposing portrait of a young monarch sitting at the end of the carpet, her brown hair crowned with a radiant tiara, her gaze unflinching, her white gown adorned with medals, and a cerulean sash that slashed across her chest like a banner of solemn authority. Goosebumps rose on my arms at the mere thought that Queen Elizabeth the Second had approved this honour. On the stage in front of the portrait stood the governor general of New Zealand. Although small in stature, she had a commanding presence, wearing a grey trouser suit adorned with multiple honorary insignia. She possessed a wide welcoming smile and seemed eager to recognise us for our "outstanding service to the Crown and to the people of New Zealand".

As I took my first step, I caught sight of my husband, Matt, my parents, my brother, my son, and other family members smiling proudly at me. Rawiri, the Māori man from my dream, was there, holding his ceremonial carved walking stick. Laurie, his daughter, was steps ahead of me on the red carpet, dressed in her family's Korowai, ready to receive her own honour.

I continued along, thinking about the brilliant bright light that I had seen in my dream years earlier, wondering what that light had represented. I thought back on all my experiences over the last decade which had led me here, and I realised that this question had been answered over and over again.

Chapter 2

Awareness of Suffering and Injustice

As a little girl in England, I loved exploring the countryside, with its patchwork of lush, green fields and its neat hedgerows and ancient woodlands begging for a game of hide and seek. Being the only girl amongst five brothers, the only way I could keep up was to roughen up my soft edges by traipsing through the mud and building dens.

My parents were loving, devoted, and hardworking. They filled our weekends with bike rides, walks, picnics, and games. We spent our summer vacations camping all over Europe, where we met and played with children of different nationalities. We celebrated our birthdays with homemade cakes, gifts, and party games. We spent Christmases with extended family, singing carols, reading the Nativity, and exchanging gifts. At Easter, we enjoyed egg hunts, special Sunday services, and hot cross buns with their delightful cinnamon, nutmeg, and an ever-so-subtle citrus taste.

Each Monday evening, my parents took us to the local sweet shop, where they gave each of us a small paper bag to fill with penny sweets. Once back home, we excitedly covered the living room floor with pillows and began jumping over our dad's back for as long as he could take it! On Sundays, we attended church, where we learned good moral values.

My parents opened our home to many children from troubled and dysfunctional backgrounds. Being a young girl, I sometimes resented having to share my bedroom and toys with these children who smelled poorly and behaved differently. One girl was particularly difficult. Standing at the kitchen window with my father, I watched this girl kicking a tree in our garden and screaming at the top of her lungs. I turned to my dad and asked, "What is wrong with that girl?" "Kerry, there is nothing wrong with her," he replied. "It's just that she's hurting a lot inside." My dad's answer led me to pause and taught me the importance of seeking to understand.

Mum and Dad brought history alive for my siblings and me by taking us to historic properties such as castles, cotton mills, large estates, and workhouses. Exciting stories of royalty, knights, princesses, and battles of bravery and triumph fascinated me. Other stories—about dungeons, poverty, and injustice—troubled me. I remember feeling disappointed and shocked when I learned of the disparity between those working in cotton mills and workhouses and those living in castles and large estates. I was especially saddened when I heard about little children who had been forced to work long hours in dangerous and harsh conditions, rarely seeing sunlight, while the landed gentry lived in ease and abundance.

My siblings and I loved it when our parents read books to us. The books included fairy tales, adventure, fiction, novels, poetry, and history. I remember my mum reading a book titled *My Lady of the Chimney Corner*, which described the aftermath of the Irish potato famine and the British people's harsh treatment of the Irish. My mother, being Irish, struggled to contain her emotions as she read each page out loud. I can still picture her sitting on a pink chair in the living room, with a box of tissues beside her. After she finished one chapter, she took us into our small garage and asked us to imagine our family living in that dark, cold, and damp place. My siblings and

I stood there soaking in the reality that those Irish people lived in terrible conditions whilst also facing starvation.

When our family watched the television series *Roots*, which was set during and after the era of slavery in the United States, I often covered my eyes. I did not want to see people being chained, assaulted, and degraded. I grappled with the fact that slavery was once legal. How could this be? But it also inspired me to learn about the early reformers who made it their mission to end slavery.

As I grew older, my awareness of suffering and injustice increased when, while setting the table for dinner, I was shocked to see a televised news report showing images of Romanian orphans subjected to institutionalised neglect and severe physical abuse. I struggled to reconcile my life with the pictures of those children. Was I even living on the same planet as them?

Anxious to *do something*, and with my parent's help, I contacted a charity that was delivering essential supplies to those Romanian orphans. I hand-wrote letters and delivered them to every house on my street, asking for donations of canned food. Hardly anyone on my street donated. I was shocked. Why wouldn't people of privilege give more freely to improve the plight of suffering children? One can of tomatoes or beans wasn't too much to ask, was it?

In my adulthood, I would face this challenge time and time again. The hand-written letters had been ineffective, clearly, so I would need to find other ways to advocate for those in need, by using my voice, time, resources and even becoming an author! Looking back, I can see that I was being prepared for things to come.

Chapter 3

Experience with Suffering, Injustice, and Comfort

As I approached my teen years, I suffered my own set of injustices and indignities, one of which lasted nine long months.

For some reason, a group of older girls, aged fifteen to sixteen, singled me out to be the subject of daily bullying at school. Sometimes I felt the sting of a shoe kicking me in the ankle or leg. Other times, I was shoved to the ground. If the bullies yanked my hair, I felt I had gotten off lightly. The worst was meeting them on the concrete stairs. Their goal was to trip me up and mock me as I tumbled.

This bullying continued for what seemed like an eternity. My parents were unaware of my suffering. I didn't tell them—I don't know why. I guess I tend to hold things in.

I prayed every night that the bullies would stop but they didn't. I began to question whether there was a God. The God I had been taught about was loving, knew me individually, and was concerned for my welfare. Why was he allowing this to happen to me? Why did he let bad things happen at all? Having more questions than answers, I concluded that God did not exist and was a figment of humankind's imagination.

After nine months, the bullies decided to take it one step further. One day as I walked through the school courtyard, the girls pounced on me and dragged me by the hair across the concrete. Then they hoisted me off the ground and propelled me towards the school pond. I had just enough time to take a deep breath before hitting the freezing water. As I emerged, gasping for breath, I heard roars of laughter and saw fingers pointing at me from all directions. That was when I noticed my undies were floating out of reach. Mortified and hurt, I dragged myself out of the pond.

My scalp was bleeding, I had scratches and scrapes all over my body, and I was shivering with cold and shock. I had no choice but to go to the school office and get help. This was my opportunity to finally tell on the bullies, so I took it.

The bullying ended that day, but the impact of those daily ordeals lingered in the form of low self-esteem and lack of confidence. The bullies' hurtful words, like "ugly freckle face," often replayed in my mind. One day, I decided to do something about it. I took a box of matches up to my bedroom and began trying to burn off each freckle, but I didn't get very far.

My experiences turned that old children's adage—"Sticks and stones may break my bones, but words can never hurt me"—on its head. Words may not have broken my bones, but they had certainly shattered my confidence and bruised my soul. There was another experience, which I have chosen not to detail because of its sensitive nature, which left me yearning for comfort. One night, I thought about praying for help, but I repeatedly rejected the idea. I mean, what was the point in praying to a God that didn't exist? But eventually, I blurted out a desperate prayer. At that moment, despite my doubts about God's existence, I felt like someone wrapped me in his arms and cradled me. No one else was in the room, but I knew I was *not* alone. I felt comforted, warm, loved, and at peace. I hoped this embrace would never end. It was powerful and unforgettable.

This embrace was the beginning of a *spiritual awakening* for me. I began praying for children who were mistreated, bullied, neglected, abused, living in poverty, or struggling with ill health. I prayed that they would be comforted the same way I had been comforted.

As I grew older, I altered my prayers slightly. I began to ask God how I could help those in need. In shifting my focus to include what *I* could do, I felt more connected with God, and I began to find my own inner voice.

Chapter 4

Marriage, Children, and My Inner Voice

Matt's engaging personality, love for nature, and high ideals instantly drew me in. We began dating when I was just seventeen years old. He was four years my senior, over six foot four in height, confident, and charming. My family instantly loved him.

Growing up, Matt had spent a lot of time on his grandparents' farm in beautiful Devonshire, England. The farm had stunning views over picturesque fields and Dartmoor National Park. Matt's chores included herding cattle, shearing sheep, and haymaking.

While Matt and I were dating, we spent much of our spare time at the family farm. He often drove me across the farm in his grandad's rusty old red tractor, and we walked across the fields for hours, returning to his nan's hearty meals.

Matt loved taking me to the local village market, where vendors sold fresh produce and farmers smoked their pipes. All the interesting characters of the countryside congregated there. The village fairs were a highlight too, with traditional tournaments like welly wanging—a competition to see who could throw a Wellington boot the farthest—and ferret racing.

It was in Devon, at the family farm, after only a few months of dating, where Matt and I fell in love and began discussing a future together.

Eighteen months later, we were married.

The following year, we welcomed our firstborn son into the world. He was born with health issues that required vigilant care and deprived me of a lot of sleep. I was still young, just twenty years old, but I suddenly had to grow up fast as I navigated my son's healthcare. Despite this rough start to motherhood, being a mother was (and is) a great joy and privilege.

Over the next few years, Matt and I tried for a second child. After a miscarriage, we discussed adoption. During my teen years, I had always felt like adoption would be part of my future, and I had even discussed the topic with Matt when we dated. We prayed about it and felt it was right. Once we had been vetted and were approved as prospective adoptive parents, our file was placed in the pool for expectant mothers to view. We were told that it could take years to be selected.

While we anxiously waited for an expectant mother to choose our profile, I was awakened one morning with a persistent thought—a thought that we should move to New Zealand!

Where did this thought come from? New Zealand had never been on my radar, and I knew very little about its people, history, geography, or culture. I had always imagined living in England my entire life, perhaps on a farm in a charming cottage. England was home, all I had ever known. The very idea of moving was foreign to me.

Was this just a random thought or was my inner voice guiding me? In the past, I had acted upon what people refer to as intuition, a hunch, an impression, or a gut feeling, and when I did so, I realised that my inner voice knew better than I did.

I shared these thoughts with Matt, who was equally taken aback. He too questioned why we would move to a land we had never visited and leave our family and friends. After taking time to pray, we both felt surprisingly peaceful about the move. Just as we did when we prayed about adoption, we felt this was right.

As we were packing up our belongings in preparation to sell our home, we received a call from a social worker. Our family profile had been chosen by an expectant mother! We were beyond excited. A couple of months later, we drove to the hospital, eager to welcome a newborn baby into our family. The "handover," however, was bittersweet as we witnessed firsthand the birth mother's grief and loss. In all our excitement, we had not thought about how she would handle the transition. I felt a huge sense of guilt and responsibility as she placed her baby into my arms. This has never left me.

Once home, we relished the time with our new baby, making sure all his needs were met. Our six-year-old son adored having a baby brother to love and to hold.

Then it came time for us to leave England and move to New Zealand. We felt our hearts being pulled in so many directions. We were acutely aware that this move affected more people than just us. Our families did not want us to leave.

The whirlwind of emotions made us question our move, but as we boarded the plane, an assurance settled upon us that this was meant to be. I was reminded that I should trust and follow my inner voice, even if it required travelling to the other side of the world.

Chapter 5

Embracing a New Land and a New Culture

Upon our arrival in New Zealand, we bought a home on the north shore of Auckland. Our garden was surrounded by red-flowered bottlebrush trees and frequented by native tuis and bellbirds, whose songs captivated me.

Just beyond our doorstep were many beaches, where we spent much of our time making sandcastles and swimming. Our oldest son joined the local sailing club, and Matt took up sea fishing, often bringing home fresh snapper for dinner. We spent our summers camping on the edge of Pakiri Beach, playing in the crashing waves, sliding down the dunes, and falling asleep to the sound of waves. We relished this laid-back lifestyle.

New Zealand's coast is lined with beautiful pohutukawa trees whose striking red flowers bloom during Christmastime. Its mountains, lakes, and forests are just as remarkable. New Zealanders love what they refer to as "the bush". The bush is the native forest where tall trees tower above shrubs and younger trees. Beneath these are ferns and mosses, which, to me, look like a wild Jurassic forest.

We found the people of New Zealand, also known as Kiwis, to be genuine, down-to-earth, and welcoming. In fact, when we first arrived, one neighbour went to great lengths to catch a live crayfish, proudly presenting it to us as a welcome gift. We had never been given a live crayfish before and didn't know what to do with it. We filled the sink with water to keep it alive until we formed a plan (I didn't like the thought of killing it). A few hours later, we found the crayfish dead in the sink. As aliens to this new land, we didn't appreciate that New Zealand crayfish live only in saltwater. It was obvious we had many lessons to learn. We quickly adopted the New Zealanders' everyday sayings. We began to say "sweet as'" because it was used instead of phrases such as "no worries," "it's all good," "take your time" and "you're welcome". We adopted "choice" in place of "brilliant" or "fantastic". Rather than "all will be well" or "everything will work out," we substituted "she'll be right". I delighted in hearing the Kiwis intertwine the Māori language with their everyday greetings and conversations. Certain Māori words became part of our vocabulary: *kia ora*, meaning "hello;" *whanau*, meaning "family;" and *aroha*, meaning "love".

I admired how the Māori respected Mother Earth, feeling a deep connection to her. I was drawn to their culture: music, dance, and many traditions that demonstrate a deep spirituality. One tradition, called a *hongi*, caught my attention. It is a greeting of touching foreheads and noses together, allowing one another to share the same breath. They view it as a way of connecting and seeing one another on a deeper level. Unbeknownst to me, I would one day be privileged to use this greeting with hundreds of children.

Chapter 6

Learning to Follow My Inner Voice

Within the first two years of living in New Zealand, our family expanded again and we welcomed a third son. During the pregnancy, I had been extremely sick and had lost hearing in my right ear. Going from two children to three was even more challenging with just one working ear and loud ringing caused by tinnitus, but I have fond memories of those days. They were busy but fun!

Despite all the chaos whilst caring for our young children, I continued to have moments when my inner voice spoke to me. On one occasion, that voice urged me to take quick action.

I breathed in the crisp sea air as my friend, Dominique, and I walked and talked on Muriwai Beach that day. The ebony sand, lush green foliage, and deep blue waters were captivating. Above us circled gannet birds, who choose the steep coastal cliffs for their nesting grounds. I thought about how New Zealand's rugged beauty possessed a different kind of allure than my homeland of England—more wild, diverse, and vast.

My friend and I glanced back to see that our husbands were still trailing far behind us. Ahead, our children ran happily along the beach. Suddenly, I got distracted by an unsettling feeling. My attention soon turned to an expectant mother and her two young children playing in the shallow surf. For some reason, I sensed they were in danger, and I had the distinct impression that they should move away from the shoreline.

I looked out at the ocean and up at the sky, wondering where this supposed danger was coming from. Nothing looked out of the ordinary. I saw no logical reason to warn her. I tried to shrug off the impression, deciding it was just a random thought. Within seconds, the impression came again, this time even stronger. A tug-of-war began: logic telling me to ignore the impression, my heart encouraging me to follow it. Logic won, and I walked past the mother and her children.

One step, two steps, three steps, four . . . another impression came. This time it consumed me. I couldn't fight it any longer. My heart won. I turned to Dominique and said, "Dom, I know this sounds strange, but I need to walk back and speak to that woman we just passed. I keep getting the feeling that she and her children are in danger." Dom gave me a bewildered expression and watched as I approached the expectant mother.

I had no idea how to start this conversation, so began with a simple "hello" and asked how her day was going. After an awkward exchange, I blurted out, "I think you need to move away from the water's edge and head back to the dunes." She stared at me with confusion written all over her face and asked, "Why?" I said the first thing that came to my mind, "There are poisonous jellyfish close to shore." She began looking into the water, searching for jellyfish, and replied with a polite "thank you". I walked away feeling very embarrassed, especially since Dominique had observed the whole awkward conversation. I left the beach with no intention of looking back.

Once the beach was out of sight, Dom asked, "Are there really poisonous jellyfish in the water?"

"Honestly, I have no idea," I replied. "I just got an overwhelming feeling that this family was in danger." Intrigued, Dom began to ask another question but was interrupted by my husband calling out to us, "Hey, you'll never believe what just happened!"

Matt described a huge wave that had just hit the beach. He and Dom's husband had seen a pregnant woman waist-deep in water, struggling to hold on to her two young children. They had hurried over to assist them. "If she had been at the water's edge, she and her children would have been swept away!" Matt exclaimed.

Dom and I looked at one another as it dawned on us that this rogue wave had been the danger I had felt. She turned to Matt and her husband and proceeded to recount what we had just experienced.

I stood there feeling relieved that the mother had listened to my warning, but I also felt some regret that I had let logic win twice. I shuddered at the thought of how different the ending of this story would have been if I had let logic win the third time.

Over time, as I received and acted upon more impressions from my inner voice, which in my faith is referred to as the Spirit, I discovered a pattern. When the first impression came, I would dismiss it as a random thought. I guess that's human nature, right? When the second impression came, I would stop and question its reason. When the third impression came, I knew that I needed to act, despite how illogical it seemed.

This pattern became especially evident one beautiful summer day at home.

I had planned to take our boys out for the afternoon. As I was going about my preparations, I decided to get a loaf of bread out of the freezer, which was in the garage, separate from the main house. As I approached the front door to go outside, I had a distinct impression not to open the front door. It took me by surprise. I ignored it and went to open the door again but received the same impression. I paused and thought about how illogical this was—we lived in a safe rural area. Once again, I went to open the door, but this time the still small voice was loud and clear, "DO NOT OPEN THE FRONT DOOR." I gasped, knowing something was off. Then another impression came, "Lock the doors, close the blinds, and gather together your children." I did it without hesitation.

My eldest son questioned what I was doing, and I explained my impression to him. I then telephoned Matt at work to relay the impressions I had received. While I was still on the phone, my son exclaimed that there was a police helicopter right above the house. "Hang up the phone and call the police," Matt said. I did so immediately. The police explained that some criminals had stolen a car and crashed next to our property. They were high on drugs and hiding behind our garage.

"I need you to gather your children inside, lock the doors, shut the blinds, and wait until the danger is over," the officer said. It hit me that these were the same instructions I had received from the Spirit just minutes earlier. I put a movie on for the kids and sat there strangely calm, despite the commotion outside. I felt reassured that my family and I were being protected and that I did not need to be afraid. A peaceful feeling rested upon me. Within twenty minutes, the police informed me that the danger was over and that we could carry on as usual.

Carry on as usual? How was I to do that? I knew that this experience, similar to that of the rogue wave, had been life-changing. I was learning the importance of following impressions from the Spirit, despite how random or out of the blue they might seem. After all, I was simply going to get a loaf of bread. How was I to know that danger was lurking just beyond the front door?

These significant experiences helped me discern the difference between a random thought and an inspired impression. I believe they were a training ground for me, prior to my dreams, teaching me to trust, follow, and take action.

Chapter 7

The First Dream

THE REVERED NEW ZEALANDER, CAPTAIN FRANK WORSLEY, NAVIgated the *Endurance* during the Imperial Trans-Antarctic expedition led by Sir Ernest Shackleton. Historians acknowledge Worsley as the key player in the crew's survival after the *Endurance* was crushed by ice floes in the Weddell Sea. His direction of a rescue party over 1300 kilometers through unforgiving waves and tempestuous winds was recognised as "an astonishing feat of navigation".

Amazingly, Frank Worsley became the captain of the *Endurance* because of an "absurd dream". Worsley's dream has been little known or acknowledged in the stories recounted of that famous journey in 1922.

In this dream, Worsley saw himself navigating a ship through Burlington Street in London. Instead of cobblestones, the street was peppered with icebergs. The day following his dream, he walked to Burlington Street where he saw a sign advertising Shackleton's expedition. Because the advertisement mentioned Antarctica, he couldn't help but connect it to the icebergs he had seen on that same street in his dream. He immediately set up a meeting with Shackleton. After only a few minutes into the interview, Shackleton appointed him captain of the *Endurance.*

During the expedition, the Endurance ended up getting stuck in ice. Worsley's dream of icebergs became a reality. He volunteered to be in the rescue party, where his navigational skills were put to the test. Worsley led them safely to the island of South Georgia, where they had to hike thirty-six hours through harsh terrain and extreme weather. Eventually, they were able to reach the whaling station to raise the alarm for the stranded crew. Captain Frank Worsley was crucial to the success of the rescue. And to think that Worsley became the Captain of the *Endurance* because of a dream!

"To each, there comes in their lifetime a special moment when they are figuratively tapped on the shoulder and offered the chance to do a very special thing." Winston Churchill once observed. I believe that Frank Worsley was tapped on the shoulder by a dream about icebergs. In my view, that "tap on the shoulder" comes when one receives their life's *calling*—a calling to do something good.

My journey didn't consist of ice floes, unforgiving waves, or a gruelling trek, but it presented itself with many personal struggles and challenges.

My tap on the shoulder came through three dreams.

I experienced my first dream after an ordinary evening of homework, dinner, bath time, stories, and prayers before getting our children to bed. When I rested my head on the pillow, I had no idea that by morning my outlook and focus would be forever changed. What I *saw* and how it propelled me to take *action* was life-changing.

In my dream, I saw thousands and thousands of children standing in front of me. I knew I was dreaming, yet it all felt so real as if I were still wide awake. As I looked into the children's eyes, I perceived that hunger dominated their every thought. They were worrying about where their next meal would come from and *if* any meal would come at all. These children were irritable, sad, and anxious. Some were even fighting with one another. My last pregnancy taught me that hunger physically hurts and also plays havoc on emotions. I saw that they were struggling physically and emotionally, but unlike my pregnancy, their hunger pains did not have a "due date".

Until this dream, I had no knowledge of any child going hungry in New Zealand. Agriculture and food production were the country's largest sources of income, so I assumed, with this abundance, that hunger did not exist. The scene unfolding in front of me showed that I assumed wrong.

This scene became particularly distressing when I discovered that a large number of these children had lost hope. At that moment, my understanding of their circumstances expanded. They had no idea of their worth. *If only they knew about this dream,* I thought, *and how God was giving me a glimpse into their lives.* To this day, the hopelessness I saw still brings me to tears.

A crushing weight of responsibility came over me like nothing I had ever felt before. This was followed by a feeling of immense love for each of these children. It was love of the purest kind: unconditional, immovable, infinite, and all-encompassing. Similar to that of a mother's love. A distinct impression came into my mind: *Feed the children.* That is when I noticed baskets, overflowing with food, at my feet. After letting out a huge sigh of relief, I eagerly began distributing the food, making sure no child was left unfed. As I did so, I looked into their eyes, at their little faces, which became etched on my soul, and expressed my love to each of them. This was no small task, but once I had fed every single child, a calmness, and peace came over me.

The once-distressing scene became a joyous one. As hunger no longer consumed their thoughts, the children began playing happily with one another. Those who had been fighting were now hugging each other. Hope had been restored! My heart overflowed with joy.

When I realised that the dream had come to an end, I didn't want to wake up for fear of forgetting the children's faces. I made a promise to myself that when I woke up, I would make it my mission to find and feed those children.

Upon stirring, I wiped away my tears and quickly scribbled down what I saw and felt. I knew I had been tapped on the shoulder and had received a *calling* that night. It was only five o'clock in the morning, so I had to wait two more hours to share the dream with Matt. He woke up to me sitting above him crying! "Do you trust me?" I asked. "Yes," he groggily replied but seemed confused and perplexed by the question. At this, I filled him in on the dream and that I would need to use our family savings to make a start. He agreed.

In the days and months that followed my dream, I thought about people who had acted on callings they received. I wondered if Dr. Martin Luther King literally had "a dream" that led him to describe his vision that "little Black boys and Black girls will be able to join hands with little white boys and white girls as sisters and brothers"?[1] Did Mahatma Gandhi dream on the night when he completely altered his life's direction and purpose, with a determination to end racial discrimination in India? Maybe. But I was not Dr. Martin Luther King or Mahatma Gandhi, and I doubted my ability to undertake the task I had been given.

The reality was that my young family and I were fairly new to this land. We had no connections in the wider community, so searching for children I had seen only in my dreams seemed impossible. We were also busy raising our three young boys and had recently been approved to adopt another child. With my limited time and resources, how could I *feed the children*?

1. Martin Luther King, "I Have a Dream", in *A Testament of Hope: The Essential Writings and Speeches of Martin Luther King Jr.*, ed. James Melvin Washington (1986), 219.

Chapter 8

Second Dream

A FEW MONTHS LATER, AFTER ANOTHER "ORDINARY" EVENING, I HAD a second lucid dream. I saw the same children I had seen in my first dream. A wave of guilt and regret came over me as I looked into each child's face. I had been given a calling to *feed the children,* but I had done nothing about it.

I had failed them.

Their struggle with hunger continued to take its toll on them, both physically and emotionally. As I began to reproach myself, an impression came again to *feed the children*, this time with even greater urgency than before.

I did not see baskets overflowing with food at my feet, as I had in my first dream. This time I saw myself working hard in various kitchens, preparing food. I worked tirelessly, and I wasn't alone. Others worked alongside me. We were all focused and driven by the task at hand. I watched as we cooked meals, packaged them, and placed them in boxes. I paid attention to each step of the process, believing that I would be doing this one day. I watched as we delivered the meals to schools. This surprised me. *Why schools? Surely the educational system provides subsidised and free lunches for children who need them.* Once again, this dream was challenging my assumptions.

The children at the schools happily ate their meals and chatted excitedly with one another. Like the first dream, this scene brought me great joy. Upon waking, I was confident that this calling was meant for *me,* despite my limitations, busy family life, and lack of resources and connections.

As I pondered my calling to feed hungry children, I thought about my dad. He was raised in England with ten other siblings. Hunger was one of the struggles he and his family had faced. He remembers one occasion when his loving mother desperately searched the kitchen cupboards for something to give her hungry children. All she found was some cooking fat and a meagre amount of bread. She sobbed as she portioned this out amongst her crying children. This early experience had a profound effect on my dad. I wish I could reach back in time to that moment, hug the child version of my dad, put a warm roll in his pocket, and fill my grandmother's cupboards with food.

My dad vividly remembers his first government-funded school meal, when the "dinner ladies" filled his plate with delicious food and offered him a second helping and pudding. "I felt like I had died and gone to heaven," he said.

Is it a coincidence that my dad did well in the subjects *after* his school lunch? I didn't think so.

I had a flashback of the children's faces from my dreams and had a better appreciation of how difficult school must be on an empty belly. It would be nearly impossible for them to concentrate, learn, and play when hunger dominated their every thought. Would they, like my dad, go home to bare kitchen cupboards? Would their mothers, like my grandmother, tearfully scrape out what little sustenance they had and distribute it amongst hungry children?

Despite having no experience forming or directing a charity, no funding options, and no influential connections, I was ready to give this calling my all. I racked my brain for ideas on how to make a start. Operating something on this scale required skills, knowledge, funds, and connections, which I did not have. I hadn't attended university. I had no degree.

After much thought, I decided to set up a catering business with the intention of using my earnings to cover the cost of lunches for children in need. Although my husband believed in my dreams, he was nervous about using our family savings to build a kitchen and take on a lease, but he reluctantly agreed. We secured a lease of a unit in a small business park on the north side of Auckland and installed a kitchen there. All my hopes to feed the children hinged on the success of this catering business.

The catering business was suddenly put on hold when my husband and I received a life-changing phone call. A birth mother had chosen our family to adopt her newborn baby girl! We were over the moon to welcome her into our family. And, as it happened, we developed a close bond with our daughter's birth family which we relished!

I had always enjoyed being a stay-at-home mum, and I cherished this time with our new daughter. During this precious time, I resented those dreams. How could I juggle my responsibilities as a full-time mum with my dreams about feeding other children?

Three months later, with the help from a close friend, Elaine, the catering business began. Elaine had been one of the first people to introduce herself to our family at church when we first arrived in New Zealand. She soon became an integral part of the business. Elaine and I made sushi, sandwiches, crackers, cookies, and muffins and sold them in the surrounding areas. The cooking, baking, cleaning, and deliveries with a baby in tow proved tricky. Getting back to collect our other children from school was a continual race against the clock.

Given the nature of my dreams, I had assumed that everything would fall into place. I naively thought that the business would automatically be a success if I worked hard enough and relied on God. However, despite an increase in orders over the next six months, there was also an increase in debt. Other challenges included leaky containers, unreliable suppliers, ever-changing delivery times, and even a brush with a drug bust.

One day, while Elaine and I were working in the newly built kitchen, I received a strong impression that we needed to move from that unit as soon as possible. I told Elaine about the impression. A few minutes later, while I was taking the rubbish to bins outside, a neighbouring business owner walked up to me with a concerned look on his face. He was usually very friendly, helpful, and jovial, despite his tough exterior.

With a pained look, he said, "Kerry, you need to leave this place."

"Why?" I frowned. "Let's just say that I've been looking out for you, but I can't anymore. It's better if you leave this place. That's all I can say."

He told me that he was part of a gang, and then he lifted his t-shirt to reveal a big tattoo of the gang's name. Awkwardly, my eyes travelled from one side of his chest to the other as I read. "That's a nice name. I haven't heard of that gang before."

I chuckle when I think back on my reaction! Although, to be fair, it's not every day that a neighbour lifts his shirt so you can read a tattoo emblazoned on their chest.

I was bewildered, so I simply thanked him and walked back to the kitchen. Elaine had overheard part of the conversation and was perplexed too. Why would we need protecting? Protection from whom? But it seemed ominous, especially considering my impression just minutes earlier. So, we knew that once again, we had to search for another rental unit.

A week later, while still in the same unit, Elaine and I heard shouting and commotion outside. Through the window, we saw a group of angry men. We heard banging, swearing, and shattering glass. A surge of panic and vulnerability came over us, and we immediately locked our door, closed our blinds, and waited. Soon we heard police sirens. When we next looked out, everyone had disappeared. Although the danger was over, we knew we could no longer delay moving. It turned out that there had been increasing tension between two local gangs, one of which the friendly shop owner belonged to. We also found out that two other unit neighbours were running meth labs, and another neighbour turned out to be posing as a policeman to keep the neighbouring businesses from being suspicious. Elaine and I had been completely unaware that we had been sharing leftover baked goods with active criminals!

Chapter 9

Third Dream

During a period of upheaval and transition, while moving both our family into a new home and the business into a new rental unit, I had a third dream. It differed significantly from the first two dreams.

In this dream, I was walking into a New Zealand government building. The building had polished floors and elegant furnishings. Many smartly dressed people congregated and talked with one another in the foyer.

I remember asking myself, "Why am I here?"

"Because of your work with feeding hungry children," came the distinct reply.

I was blown away. It left me imagining the impact of feeding hungry children—so much that I would be invited here. Was everyone here to discuss how the government could implement food in schools? Whatever the reason, I knew it was significant.

I then noticed a Māori man looking directly at me. He was holding a large set of keys. He beckoned for me to walk towards him, and as I did so, he began opening a large, walnut-coloured wooden door with his keys. Once the door was open, I noticed a brilliant bright light shining just beyond, and he gestured for me to walk through the door. As I walked through and into the light, my dream ended.

I sat up in bed and scribbled down the details of the dream. I was confident that one day I would find and feed the hungry children, meet the Māori man who had unlocked the door for me, and be invited to that very same government building.

Chapter 10

An Extraordinary Conversation

I HAD TO TAKE A SECOND LOOK. WAS IT REALLY HIM? INCREDIBLY, IT was! It was the Māori man from my dream. He and I were attending the same conference. We were strangers, yet I felt I knew him. I wanted to tell him the unbelievable fact that he had been in my dream, but I feared he would think me crazy. Instead, I found out his name and contact details, thinking I would wait for a better time to tell him.

Was there really a better time to share something as peculiar as this?

A few months after the conference, my family and I travelled to visit our daughter's birth family. As we tackled busy traffic, I saw a green area next to the highway, where some buildings stood. Out of the blue, I had the impression that the children from my dreams were in this area. I burst into tears, asking my husband where we were. We were passing South Auckland. It had been two years since my initial dream, and finally I knew where the children were. At that moment, I knew I must call the Māori man I had seen in my third dream. His name was Rawiri. How would I even start the conversation?

As I dialled his phone number, my heart began thumping out of my chest. He answered, and I plunged ahead awkwardly.

"Hi . . . so umm . . . this is Kerry Owen; you don't know me, but . . ."

"Are you Pakeha?" Rawiri asked. (Pakeha is a Māori term for "white".)

"Yes," I said.

"Are you blonde?" he asked, as though he were trying to draw a mental image of me in his brain. "Yes. I have highlights, but yeah, kind of . . ." I stumbled through.

There was a brief pause, filled with relief. "I have been waiting for your call for some time now." That statement left me speechless. How could he have been waiting for my call? We were strangers! I racked my brain, thinking of any possible reason he'd been expecting my call. Finally, I was able to speak again. "Umm . . . did you have a dream about me?"

"Yes, some time ago. I have been waiting for your call," he said.

I paused, shocked by what I was hearing. "Really? Can you tell me what you dreamed about?"

"I saw a Pakeha blonde woman in my dream. I saw you holding a baby."

"Yes, we adopted a little girl."

"I was told she was going to help our tamariki."

"What does *tamariki* mean?" I asked.

"Children." He continued as though he hadn't just dropped a bombshell. "And that she was also going to help their hauora."

I swallowed hard. "What does *hauora* mean?"

"Health and well-being."

"Wow." I was stunned. I found myself pacing around the room, trying to process that Rawiri had seen me in a dream, just as I had seen him in *mine*. The message about children and their health and well-being was in *his* dream, just like *mine*. Instead of being anxious about sharing my dreams with him, I was excited! This was no coincidence.

Rawiri went on to explain that in his dream, he had questioned, "How was a Pakeha woman going to help our tamariki?"

"She has a good heart," he was told. At this point, tears were running down my cheeks. The words "she has a good heart" struck me to the core, and I felt completely undone. Rawiri continued, "I'm not sure what you will do, but I know I am to open doors for you. I saw you walking in a government building, and I was holding keys. I opened a door for you, and beyond that door was a bright light."

If I was stunned before, now I am dumbfounded. Rawiri had not only received the same messages in his dream but had also seen the same images: the government building, the keys, the door, and the light. This validated my dreams in a way nothing else could.

Within days of our enlightening phone call, Rawiri and his wife visited Matt and me. As Rawiri entered our home, my eyes were instantly drawn to the walking stick he was using. It was evident that it was no ordinary walking stick. It had intricate patterns and fine details carved into it. I later learned that it was a *tokotoko*, a ceremonial carved walking stick that represented Rawiri's status as a *Kaumatua* (respected leader in the Māori community) and his *mana* (strength, pride, and identity).

Once Rawiri began to speak, a feeling of reverence entered the room. I was glad that Matt was able to hear Rawiri's dreams firsthand. We all concluded that these dreams were divinely inspired and that I had been called to feed the children in our adopted land of New Zealand.

We discussed what I had done so far, such as taking on a lease, installing a kitchen, and running a catering company in order to fund the charitable lunches.

Rawiri told us that he worked in the field of Māori health and had worked with government officials to improve care for the Māori people. Since Rawiri had been holding keys in my dream, I assumed and even hoped that he would take the reins of leadership and be able to give me clear instructions on how to feed the children. I suggested that perhaps he was meant to lead this work, but he was adamant that this was not the case. His role was to open doors.

Rawiri's visit brought validation that Matt seemed to need. Matt was supportive of my efforts to follow my dreams, but sometimes he became frustrated with the demands on my time and the drain on our finances. In those moments, he often said, "Kerry, I did not have your dreams." It was good to now have Matt completely on board, recognising that my dreams were indeed inspired and understanding that his support and participation would be crucial on this journey.

Chapter 11

Adopting 183 Children

It had been four years since the initial dream, and a lot had transpired! My four children were aged two, seven, nine, and fourteen. We had moved the catering business twice and were now operating a busy café. Finally, I was in a position to "feed the children".

My friend and co-worker Elaine believed in my dreams and my *calling* to feed. She later said, "There was always a goal, and that end goal for Kerry was the charity. So off she went, flying to fulfil her dreams."

In my eagerness to get started with the charitable lunches, I began calling schools in South Auckland, hoping a school would agree to a trial programme. I was so disappointed to be met with resistance and people who questioned my intentions. How could I make a start if no one would give me a chance to serve?

Upon hearing about my predicament, Rawiri spoke with a school principal he knew. This principal led a school known as a *kura*, based on immersion in Māori practices and philosophies. The principal was open to the idea, as his students came from low socioeconomic backgrounds, but he explained that it would require the school board's approval first.

Rawiri arranged for me to speak at the next *kura* board meeting, but I was hesitant. I wasn't Māori. I didn't speak Te Reo Māori. I wasn't even a New Zealander. I wasn't an experienced speaker. I was not many things! I was simply a woman who'd had dreams and was working on making them a reality. What could I say to persuade this board? Rawiri felt strongly that I should share my dreams with the board. Share my dreams? With a group of strangers? *No way*, I thought, knowing full well that sharing dreams is viewed as an oddity! As I thought about sharing my dreams with a room full of strangers, panic set in.

Rawiri, seeing my panic, suggested I pray about it. As I did so, a peaceful feeling came over me. That same evening, I went to the board meeting with Rawiri and his daughter Laurie. Laurie and I met shortly after my initial meeting with Rawiri because he had felt a synergy between Laurie's background and my calling to *feed the children*. Laurie had studied human nutrition and worked in indigenous public health. Little did she or I know that she would eventually become an essential part of the work ahead.

Upon our arrival at the *kura*, we were invited to sit at the front of the room while the board conducted their general business. The meeting was conducted in Te Reo Māori, so I didn't understand a word. Rawiri was then invited to speak. He shared a few words in Te Reo Māori and then gestured for me to stand. My apprehension about sharing my dreams in public returned. Very awkwardly, I began.

Initially, the board seemed disinterested in what I had to say. That changed when I started sharing my dreams. People began leaning forwards in their chairs, and some had tears well up in their eyes. When I had finished speaking, there was complete silence.

The feeling in the room was beautiful.

The people seemed deep in their thoughts while acknowledging me with eye contact and warm smiles. It was during this silence that it dawned on me. Rawiri had figuratively opened a door for me into his culture and his people. Beyond that door lay an opportunity to learn, love, be loved, and serve.

Rawiri knew that his people would understand and connect with my dreams. This was an unforgettable teaching moment. It was the first of many moments in which I learned that the Māori people have a natural affinity for dreams, impressions, and things of a spiritual nature. Although I wasn't speaking in Te Reo Māori, I was speaking a spiritual language they understood.

After I finished speaking, the principal stood up, thanking me for sharing my "powerful story". He concluded by exclaiming, "Kerry, we are happy for you to do a trial at our kura. Congratulations! You have now adopted our 183 students!" The word *adopted* struck an emotional chord with me, given that my husband and I had adopted two children. I was touched and honoured that the principal used this particular word in relation to the children of the kura.

I realised that as I ventured through this open door and into this new culture, I would need to stretch myself beyond my reserved nature and be willing to share what was in my heart and soul.

Chapter 12

Miracles

In a remote part of New Zealand, a young, inexperienced doctor once faced a situation for which he was unprepared. An eight-year-old boy had sustained a life-threatening head injury, and his only chance for survival was immediate invasive surgery. The young doctor had never witnessed a brain surgery, let alone performed one, but he was the only doctor there.

He said a fervent prayer; then it became a case of all hands on deck. A policeman administered the anaesthetic, a nurse became the surgical assistant, and the work began with the most basic surgical instruments under a small light. A neurosurgeon from the north island of New Zealand helped the young doctor over the telephone. Unfortunately, FaceTime and Zoom weren't available then.

The doctor said he felt an unseen power aiding him during the surgery, providing him guidance and comfort. After six long hours, the surgery was complete and a huge success. This young doctor was convinced a miracle had occurred. Some might say the eight-year-old boy's life was saved because of the young doctor's careful and precise work or perhaps because of the neurosurgeon's help over the phone. Of course, both played important roles, but decades later, the now-retired doctor is still as adamant as ever that a miracle occurred that night. How do I know this? Because this doctor, Neil, was my doctor before he retired.

Shortly after Neil retired, I was admitted to the hospital for surgery. The surgery went well, but the recovery proved difficult. I remember laying in my hospital bed, wishing Neil could visit with me, but I knew he was travelling across New Zealand, enjoying his retirement. Minutes after having this thought, there was a knock on my hospital room door, and in walked Neil! I could not believe my eyes, and I burst into tears. "How did you know I was here?" I asked. Neil explained that he'd received an impression to check up on me, completely unaware that I had had surgery. He telephoned my home number, only to find out that I was in the hospital. What a comfort his visit was!

I believe Neil had a *calling* to be a doctor, and because he submitted to that calling, he experienced miracles along his life's journey. My call to feed the children was also accompanied by miracles. The first miracle came in the form of baked potatoes. Yes, that's right: potatoes!

On the first day of the charitable lunch trial at the kura, the principal invited me, Laurie—Rawiri's daughter—and Rawiri, along with a group of volunteers, to a special school assembly. He wanted to introduce the children to us, tell them about the trial lunch programme, and give us a formal welcome. To ensure we had adequate time to prepare the food and attend the assembly, he allowed us to use the school kitchen that first day. For the rest of the trial programme, we would use the café kitchen that I was already operating.

Before the assembly, our group of volunteers washed 183 potatoes, turned on the kura's large oven, and placed the potatoes in the oven. We went to the assembly hall, thinking that the potatoes would be almost done cooking by the time we returned to the kitchen.

In the assembly hall, the principal warmly introduced us and explained the lunch programme. In an expression of gratitude, the students performed a Māori song called a *kapa haka*. Then they lined up and did a *hongi* with each of us. In a hongi, two people press their noses and foreheads together and breathe in. They exchange the *ha,* or breath of life, in a symbolic show of unity. No words were said as we did hongi with all 183 children, but the feeling of unity was compelling. I will always treasure that privilege. I had loved learning about the hongi when we first arrived in New Zealand, but I had never imagined I would experience it in such a meaningful way.

Once the assembly ended, we walked back to the kitchen and opened the oven door only to find the oven cold and the potatoes uncooked. The potatoes had been in there for over ninety minutes. We were scheduled to begin serving in forty-five minutes. We couldn't serve the children raw potatoes!

Our group huddled in the kitchen and prayed to find a way to feed the children on time. Laurie suggested that we approach the local *marae* and see if we could use their ovens. A marae is a Māori meeting place for celebrations, funerals, cultural events, and workshops. Everyone agreed but with a sinking feeling. We all knew the ovens wouldn't heat up and cook 183 potatoes in time. We decided to keep 30 potatoes back to boil and microwave.

Laurie and another volunteer, Jeremy, loaded the car with the other 153 potatoes and went to the local marae. Their ovens were already in use, so were directed to the nearest church. The church's ovens were available, but we were scheduled to serve the children in less than thirty minutes!

Meanwhile, back in the kura's kitchen, we were boiling potatoes in several pots. Soon enough, the children began waiting in line outside the kitchen window. We took a deep breath and began serving the boiled, disastrous-looking potatoes, adding lots of extra toppings to disguise their appearance. As the number of students in line increased, so did my blood pressure!

Silently and desperately, I prayed again for a miracle. Within minutes, Laurie and Jeremy walked in and handed us 60 large fully baked potatoes! We all stood in disbelief, staring at the potatoes and questioning how 60 large potatoes could be fully baked in less than thirty minutes. This wasn't possible, especially since the ovens needed time to heat up first. Nevertheless, here they were, hot and beautifully baked!

With much relief, we gladly began filling the potatoes with toppings and sending them out to the students waiting in line. Jeremy left and soon returned with the remaining fully baked potatoes. We all knew we had witnessed a miracle!

Once we had finished serving the lunches, our team huddled again together, this time to offer a prayer of thanks. It was a day to remember. "As we scrambled, begged, baked, and sweated, a miracle occurred that I will never forget. Baking those large potatoes in less than thirty minutes defied the laws of physics," Laurie said.

Year after year, we witnessed similar miracles. Once, after having cooked large pots of fresh hot soup, the volunteers and I loaded the soup into upright heat warmers, and secured those heat warmers in the delivery truck. When we arrived at the school gate, we were met by hundreds of children, who were excitedly anticipating the soup and bread rolls. I remember thinking how I wished my own children were this excited when I served up soup for dinner! When we opened the truck doors, we were dismayed to find soup dripping off the ceiling, and onto the truck floor. The straps we had tied around the food warmers had snapped en route. Now we were left with only one food warmer still intact. Our hearts sank because this meant that we had only a third of the soup we needed for that day's delivery. We had 380 children to feed, but only enough soup to feed 125. The volunteers and I came together and prayed for a miracle. We needed one!

As we began handing out the soup, we noticed something quite remarkable. The soup was going further than expected..much further! By the end, we had fed all 380 children. It reminded me of a Bible story I had learned in my childhood: Jesus miraculously fed five thousand people with five loaves and two fishes.

The volunteers and I knew we had witnessed a miracle that day and gave a prayer of thanks. It was a reminder that "with God, all things are possible".

Miracles come in various forms: a young, inexperienced doctor saving someone's life; an old, experienced doctor paying an unexpected visit; 153 oven-baked potatoes; an inadequate supply of food stretching to feed hungry children. One thing all these miracles have in common is that their purpose is to help someone in need.

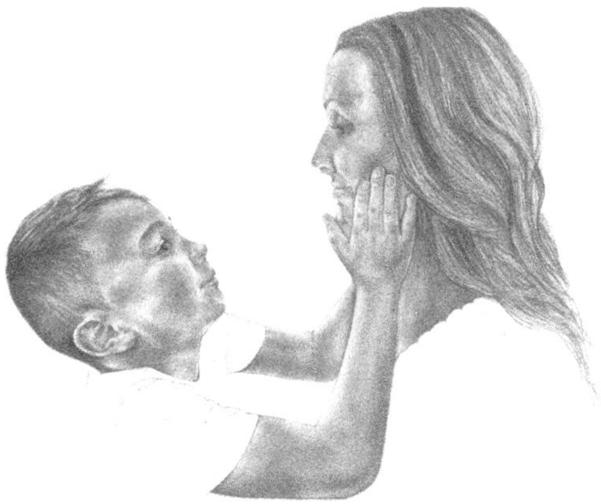

Chapter 13

Charity Work Is All About *Love*

I LOOKED INTO A SEA OF BEAMING YOUNG FACES, AND THERE HE WAS. A jolt of recognition went through me as I realised he was one of the children I had seen in my dreams years earlier.

By this time, the New Zealand Charities Commission had officially recognised my charity organisation, called Feed the Need.

We were now serving lunches in several schools. Teachers noted a marked improvement in their students' well-being, attendance, and focus in class. Prior to our lunch programme, some teachers had prepared and supplied extra sandwiches for students who came without lunch. Some had observed children with empty lunch boxes, pretending to eat alongside their friends so as not to draw unwanted attention to themselves. The teachers were grateful beyond measure for our lunch programme. On this particular day, we were invited to a school to see how our lunch programme was going. Nothing could have prepared me for the moment I met that boy. He was small, around six years old, with a beautiful dark complexion, unruly hair, and big brown eyes. Barefooted, he hurried to sit next to me and tenderly placed his hands on either side of my face.

This boy was the first of many children I would meet whom I had seen in my dreams.

As he held my face, he looked directly into my eyes with such familiarity that I wondered if he also recognised me. Had he seen me in *his* dreams?

"Are you an angel?" he asked. "I'm not an angel," I replied. "My name is Kerry."

I wanted to tell him about the dreams and to apologise for taking so long to find him, but I couldn't say a word. My emotions gave way, and tears began falling down my face. The boy gently wiped away my tears, leaned forwards, and softly said, "I love you."

Through my tears, I managed to whisper, "I love you too . . . very much." He smiled and took my hands in his.

We didn't exchange any other words, it didn't seem necessary. Sitting in each other's company was enough. For me, this meeting was not a coincidence. Wess Stafford, an advocate for children and a former CEO of Compassion International, once stated, "Every child you encounter is a divine appointment."[2]

Our time together was interrupted by the school bell indicating that lunchtime was over. The boy and I embraced, waved goodbye, and went our separate ways. As I drove home, the encounter dominated my thoughts. I cried so much that Laurie, who was my front passenger, offered to take over the steering wheel, concerned that I couldn't see the road through my tears.

"If all of this work was only meant to reach this one boy, then it was worth it!" I sobbed.

Several weeks later, I inquired about the boy's well-being. The school office staff informed me that he had moved with his mother into a women's refuge shelter several miles away. In the process, he also moved to a different school. They added that this very same boy had walked several miles barefoot in the rain back to their school, hoping

2. Wess Stafford, in "Famous Quotes about Children," Compassion International website, compassion.com/poverty/famous-quotes-about-children.htm.

to have some of our soup, despite the women's refuge shelter giving him a packed school lunch. That was when I realised that this work was about much more than filling hungry bellies. It struck me that this simple meal of soup and bread communicated to the children that people cared about them. It told them that they mattered.

Although I never met this boy again, he taught me an important lesson: to take every opportunity to tell those we serve that we love them.

A couple of years later I had another opportunity to communicate to those we served that we cared about them and loved them—this time in front of a school assembly.

A retired legend from the rugby team called the *All Blacks* had agreed to visit one of the schools we served. Laurie and I met with him and the school principal upon our arrival. The school was thrilled to have this rugby legend visit them, and they prepared a special welcome for him in the assembly hall. As the principal led us to the hall, he dropped a bombshell, telling us that 43 percent of his students were in state care. That number shocked me. He added that the school even had a social worker onsite to support those recovering from trauma. As we entered the hall, I saw hundreds of familiar faces—faces I had seen in my dreams years earlier. As I watched the students formally welcome the rugby legend with beautiful singing and dancing, a lump formed in my throat, and tears began swelling in my eyes.

Once the kapa haka had finished, the principal unexpectedly announced, "I would like to invite Kerry Owen, the founder of Feed the Need, to introduce herself." I struggled to compose myself as I stood up. I emotionally asked the students if they could tell me why Feed the Need was providing this school lunch programme. One child said, "To fill our hungry *pukus*" (tummies).

"To make us healthy," another said. Assuring them that they were both correct, I added that there was one more reason. The children were struggling to think of another reason, so I jumped in and said, "It's because everyone at Feed the Need loves you. I don't know your names or hobbies, but I love each of you. When I tuck my children into bed at night, I think about each of you and want you to know that you are loved."

There was complete silence as I made my way back to the chair at the front of the assembly hall. You could have heard a pin drop. To this day, I am unsure if it was an awkward or good silence. As I sat down, Laurie gave me a wink and whispered, "Good one," with an approving smile. Despite her assurance, I worried whether expressing my love for the children had been appropriate. Did the teachers and principal think it unprofessional?

Weeks later, I received many handmade cards from children who had attended that assembly. A card from a young girl has remained etched in my mind ever since. She had drawn a picture of me on one side of the card. I was smiling and surrounded by colourful flowers and sunshine. On the other side of the card was a drawing of a child crying in the rain, and it was in black and white; there was no colour.

On the back of this card, the young girl wrote, "When you said you loved me, no one's told me that before. It made me feel happy. I love you too. I will never forget you, never forget you, never forget you. Please don't forget me, don't forget me, don't forget me." This card was bittersweet. The words "no one's told me that before" were painful to read. On the other hand, I was grateful to have used that moment in the assembly hall to let this child feel someone's sincere love.

We should let those we serve know that we care and that they matter. As in that child's case, we might be the only person to let them know they are loved!

Chapter 14

Are You Two Sisters?

In my childhood, I had close friends of Indian and African descent. They experienced prejudice at school, which bothered and perplexed me greatly. Our different cultures and religious beliefs did not define or limit our friendships.

During my teenage years, my parents hosted students from all across the globe. I enjoyed interacting with the students and learning about their diverse cultures, food, dress, religions, and customs. My biggest takeaway from these experiences was a sense of how connected humankind is.

When I first heard New Zealand's national anthem, I was deeply moved, especially by one line: Men of every creed and race, gather here before thy face. Soon after this line was sung in English, the song switched to Te Reo Māori, the language of the indigenous people of the land. This spoke an important truth to me, conjuring up an image of unity and harmony among different races. I felt blessed to be in New Zealand, and I envisioned that I would feel at home living amongst the people there.

At that time, I had no idea of how connected I would become with the people of this land. One of these people being Laurie, Rawiri's daughter.

One day, while Laurie and I were discussing the charity, she literally gasped, leaned back in her chair, and began crying. Through her tears, she explained that she felt she was meant to be more involved with the work I was doing. She later said, "I was shown in an instant the key milestones of my life's path. My journey was no accident, and it was all to prepare me for what I was about to embark on." I was grateful that Laurie had this impression and, more importantly, that she was willing to follow it, despite having a young family herself. We became incredibly close as we served together.

While Laurie and I were delivering lunches to one of our schools, a young Māori student approached me and asked, "Are you two sisters?" Laurie being Māori and I being English, we have contrasting skin tones, eyes, hair, and height. We couldn't look more different. We also have different accents.

Initially, I chuckled. You see, the children at the schools often asked us the funniest questions. For example, I was asked many times why I had no eyebrows. I do have eyebrows, but they are fair. However, this boy stood before me and asked again, "Are you two sisters?" Realising that his question was in earnest, I paused for a moment. I thought, *Does this boy not see the obvious differences in our appearance, race, and accent? Perhaps he does see the differences, but he thinks they make no difference.* He stood there, eagerly awaiting my answer.

"We're not sisters," I replied. "We did not grow up in the same family." He seemed disappointed, but I added that we often felt like sisters as we served together. With that, he seemed content and ran off to his table.

This boy left an indelible mark on me. Why? Because his question spoke the truth. The truth I refer to is that family isn't limited to having the same genetics or appearance. Family is about LOVE.

I have since concluded that this boy must have observed Laurie and me interacting with one another. Maybe he saw us helping each other carry boxes of food or hugging one another after we had finished serving and assumed this meant we were sisters. His question is a reminder that children are always watching adults and forming opinions by what they see.

This begs a question: If this boy assumed Laurie and I were sisters, would children across the world assume we are all brothers and sisters if only we loved and served one another?

In the case of Laurie and me, our diversity brought different strengths and perspectives that made our charity work impactful. Rather than allowing our differences to divide us, we both learned to use them to do good, forming an affinity between us.

Whina Cooper, a beloved New Zealand woman who fought for Māori land rights, said, "The seed I would like to plant in your heart is a vision . . . where all our people can live in harmony . . . and share the wisdom from each culture."[3]

That young boy's question can be a lesson to us all.

---

3. Whina Cooper, quoted by Dame Claudia Orange, in "Twelve Questions: Dame Claudia Orange", NZ Herald, Feb. 3, 2016, https://www.nzherald.co.nz/kahu/twelve-questions-dame-claudia-orange/I6XOY66B3QDDKWJD4JXXYVRXFU/.

Chapter 15

Can I Quit?

In 1893, about 90,000 women walked to the polling booths across New Zealand and voted for the first time. New Zealand became the first nation in the world to allow all women to vote.

Over a decade earlier, Kate Sheppard had embarked on a mission to ensure all women in New Zealand had the right to vote. She organised rallies, marches, and campaigns across the country, where she delivered persuasive and influential speeches.[4]

One night, when all hope seemed lost, Kate contemplated giving up. However, when she tried to sleep that night, she saw the names of women who had signed the petition. She remembered their faces.[5] This experience renewed her passion and commitment to the cause.

4. See "Sheppard, Kate (1847–1934)", encyclopedia.com; "Story: Sheppard, Katharine Wilson," in Ngā Tāngata Taumata Rau: Dictionary of New Zealand Biography, https://teara.govt.nz/en/biographies/2s20/sheppard-katherine-wilson.

5. See Maria Gill and Marco Ivančić, *Kate Sheppard: Leading the way for women* (2018), 00–00..

Like Kate Sheppard, I was tempted to quit. You would think that having had such vivid and instructive dreams, I would never want to quit, but you'd be wrong.

The café and charity work were physically and emotionally demanding. I began losing an excessive amount of weight and experiencing recurring poor health. I floundered, made many mistakes, and let my family and friends down.

After a particularly challenging day, I got on my knees and prayed, begging for permission to walk away from my dreams and go back to the simpler life. I longed to be a full-time mum again and have more time with my family. I wanted to be free of our increasing debt. I was desperate for more sleep and rest. I prayed for someone else, *anyone else*, to have my dreams so I could step away.

As I fervently prayed, my perspective on my "calling" went through a significant metamorphosis. Images of people living in poverty and hardship began popping into my mind. I saw and felt their struggle.

I knew that I was not facing poverty or hardship. I was privileged in many ways, and because of this privilege, I was meant to do everything I could to help those in need. Once the images receded, I knew I had my answer.

I was not given the assurance, "It's okay, Kerry; you can walk away." But neither was I given an ultimatum, "Kerry, you have no choice; you must do this." I realised that this "call" was an invitation I had willingly accepted. It was now a part of me. If I were to walk away, I would walk away not only from those in need but also from myself. My resolve returned, and my vision was renewed.

In the Disney movie *Moana,* the title character feels a "call" to help her people. She begins a voyage across the ocean. While on this voyage, she meets many obstacles and reaches a point where she feels she can't carry on anymore. Her grandmother, who has already passed on from this life, visits her to remind her of who she is and what she's capable of. Moana's resolve is renewed. When I first saw that movie, I was reminded of the time I wanted to quit. I often reflect on that prayer and think of how different my life would have been if the answer had been, "It's okay, Kerry; you can quit now." Children would have continued to go hungry, some never knowing that they were loved and cared for. I would not have been able to advocate for them, and I would have missed out on many lessons and personal growth along the way.

Chapter 16

Meaningful Connections

ONE DAY AFTER A BUSY LUNCH HOUR AT THE CAFÉ, THE DISHES WERE piled up high and waiting to be cleaned, the walk-in refrigerator needed reorganising, and another fifty hard-boiled eggs were waiting to be peeled. Every day at the café was like this. I occasionally found myself resenting the tedious and demanding work, yet I knew it served an important purpose for Feed the Need.

On this particular afternoon, as I wiped down the tables, I noticed Allan, the CEO of the telecommunications company that occupied most of the office building where the café was located. He was still sitting at his table. He was always friendly, but the café staff and I had been told by HR to never disturb him when he was in the café, as this was his time to "unwind without any distractions".

Once I finished wiping down the tables, I walked into the kitchen through the revolving door and Elaine handed me a cup of coffee. "This is for Allan," she said. "Can you take it to him?"

At that moment, I got the distinct impression that I should talk with Allan about Feed the Need. I rejected the idea immediately.

However, within a split second, the same impression came again. I froze behind the swinging silver door that divided the café from the kitchen, still holding his coffee. I wrestled with which was worse: ignoring the impression or disturbing the CEO. The rogue wave experience came to mind, so I quickly concluded it would be worse to ignore the impression. As I placed the coffee on Allan's table, I nervously asked, "You're Allan, aren't you?"

"Yes, I am."

After I introduced myself, he smiled, saying that he already knew who I was. He warmly invited me to sit with him. With this invitation, I eagerly began to talk about the charity. He stopped me mid-sentence and asked if I could tell him a little about myself first. I gave him the usual answers: that I was married with four children and had moved from England to New Zealand.

"How many cafes have you operated before now?"

"None," I replied. With a surprised expression on his face, he asked, "How on earth did you win the contract for this cafe, having zero cafe experience? How did you know how much food you'd need to order?"

I told him that I knew something about ordering food because I had set up a catering business a couple of years earlier as a way of funding charity lunches. Elaine and I had catered to some of his employees, and shortly after were invited to take over the café situated in their office building. I had to admit that when I placed the first order of food and supplies, I was biting my nails and hoping I did not mess up on the quantities! As Allan listened to me share this story, he seemed amused. He was right to be amused; it made no logical sense. But nothing on this journey to feed the need made logical sense.

Finally, he said, "Now, tell me about this charity."

With this green light, I told him about the growing issue of food insecurity in New Zealand and how our charity food programme worked. Again, he smiled, shook his head, and asked, "So you're operating this cafe, directing the charity, and have four young children in tow? Are you crazy?"

"I guess I am!"

Allan then told me that just a week earlier, he had delivered a speech on food insecurity in New Zealand! He gave me a copy of his speech. Part of it read, "I know that unless I address the issue of children, their health, their education, their poverty, and well-being, it is going to cost my business and my shareholders in the long term. It is going to cost our society, our nation, and our souls."

I knew then it was no coincidence that I had an impression to approach Allan.

Allan and I had a meaningful exchange of thoughts and ideas, which resulted in him deciding to take me under his wing. "You will need to network to rally up support and awareness for what you are doing. I can help you with this. There are several upcoming events which you could attend to build up your network."

The thought of networking did not appeal to me. The idea of having meaningless and awkward conversations whilst constantly checking my watch for an appropriate time to leave made me cringe. "Thank you," I said, "but I don't like networking. It seems so superficial."

He nodded, paused for a moment, and replied, "Individuals who are authentic and sincere will be drawn to you, and vice versa. Networking is an effective way to connect with others, to find like-minded individuals."

When I left the room, I felt that our meeting was meant to be. I knew it would open doors for our charity. Within days of our conversation, I received the first invitation to an event.

My introverted self squirmed at the thought but accepted anyway. When I arrived, I stood to the side of the venue, awkwardly watching the attendees, who seemed to be effortlessly chatting and laughing with one another. Before long, I noticed someone near me who was drinking on her own. Was she also feeling uncomfortable?

I cannot remember whether she or I struck up the conversation, but we had a meaningful chat. Her name was Natalie, and she was a gifted writer. She offered to write the story behind Feed the Need. At the time, I did not feel comfortable telling people about my dreams. Instead, I would share a secondary story, which was also true, about my dad's struggle with food insecurity during his childhood. Natalie helped me share my complete story in a way that motivated people to contribute. We included her writing on our website. And her input did not end there. She eventually served as the board chair for Feed the Need.

Allan continued to push me out of my comfort zone. He put me forwards as a speaker at an event discussing poverty. Many leaders, including the nationwide children's commissioner, would be in attendance. I cried throughout the delivery of my speech and struggled to finish it. I felt a strong responsibility to advocate for the children we served. Afterward, the children's commissioner approached me and commended me on delivering a "very powerful speech." We ended up having a meaningful, albeit short, conversation.

Sometime later, the children's commissioner agreed to a television interview that featured Feed the Need. Because he was a leading paediatrician and the nation's children's commissioner, his interview had a significant impact on the effort to feed hungry children in New Zealand. He challenged the status quo, saying, "We are a first-world country with a temperate climate, and agriculture is the backbone of our economy. I don't understand how we can have poverty, [. . .] particularly food poverty in New Zealand. It just doesn't make sense."

He was right. New Zealand is a land of natural abundance and is frequently referred to as the land of milk and honey. It accounts for approximately 35 percent of world trade in dairy products. The children's commissioner added weight to the argument that this was a national issue. The news story ended with me pleading for help. "I am now begging the country . . . to step up and help," I said. We need to invest in these children—this should be a top priority. These children deserve the best. They are the future of New Zealand."

At another meeting, Allan noticed that I was immobilised with fear, so he playfully elbowed me right into a group of community and nationwide leaders.

This push led me to meet a leader of The Salvation Army, who concluded that working collaboratively would do much more good than working separately. Feed the Need later installed a commercial kitchen in one of their buildings. We used the kitchen for our lunch programme, and they also used it to serve the community.

Perhaps the most significant of Allan's introductions was that of Jacinda. Had I known that Jacinda would eventually become the prime minister of New Zealand, I may have been apprehensive about meeting her.

When I first conversed with Jacinda over a cup of peppermint tea, it was like settling down for a chat with an old friend. She had an open and direct style, which, combined with her warm smile, immediately set me at ease. Jacinda and I quickly discovered that we had one thing in common: a passion and drive to improve the lives of children, particularly those troubled by food insecurity.

She had developed a sense of responsibility in her former years. She spent time serving the homeless in a soup kitchen in New York. Then chose politics as her avenue of influencing change. At twenty-eight years old, she became the youngest member of the New Zealand Parliament. During our conversation, I was filled with hope that, in time, Jacinda would influence the government to take action and introduce a lunch programme within New Zealand's schools. Over the next two years, Jacinda quickly became a well-known political and public figure. One day, I got an impression to invite her to be an adviser to the Feed the Need board. Doubting that Jacinda would say yes (as various, much larger charitable organisations had already approached her), I dismissed the impression. However, the impression came again, so I ran the idea past the board. Their reaction was divided. Some felt that Jacinda's prominence as a political figure would negatively impact Feed the Need. Some felt that her passion for the topic of "food in schools" was exactly what we needed. Despite this division, my impression of inviting Jacinda continued. Eventually, the board decided to take a vote. Jacinda was elected with one stipulation: she would be a non-voting adviser.

Jacinda accepted the invitation. Despite the demands on her time from the public, the media, and the Parliament, she always made time for Feed the Need. She rolled up her sleeves, worked alongside the youth in our kitchen, visited the schools we served, and sat on concrete floors alongside young students, taking a keen interest in them.

When Jacinda Ardern was elected as prime minister of New Zealand, it did not surprise me that she read every single child's letter she received from all across New Zealand. Neither did it surprise me that Jacinda held a press conference just for children.

I am grateful to have learned that it was possible to form meaningful connections through a networking process in which I was initially reluctant to participate. As I reflect, I can see clearly that these connections were essential to the work of Feed the Need. I marvel that it began with such a small and simple thing: shakily setting down a cuppa and beginning a conversation with Allan.

Chapter 17

Unseen Help

DURING THE YEARS OF WORKING ON THE GROUND WITH FEED THE Need, I was constantly plagued with sickness. The long hours, the sleepless nights, and the physical demands took a toll on my body. Unbeknownst to me at the time, I was living with a chronic health condition called primary immunodeficiency. It wasn't until years later that I was diagnosed. I now receive immunoglobulin infusions every two weeks.

On one occasion, a national television show wanted to do a story on Feed the Need. It would require many hours of filming in the kitchen, in the schools, a sit-down interview, and a speech to one of our corporate sponsors. This was a rare opportunity. However, I had been bed-bound for a couple of months, spending my time in and out of the hospital. I asked the producer if I could have someone else speak on my behalf, but she insisted that it be me, the founder.

I faced a dilemma. If I refused, I would let go of a great opportunity to raise awareness and advocate for children going hungry. If I agreed, I would face the seemingly impossible, physically and mentally. I prayed about it, and the answer was clear: I should do it. I cried for hours knowing this would be so difficult.

Within hours of being disconnected from the IV drip at the hospital, my friend Irene drove me to the location where I was to deliver the speech. All I wanted to do was to crawl back into the hospital bed.

Upon my arrival, there were hundreds of people and a film crew waiting for me. When I reached the podium and began my speech, I was shaky, weak, and nauseous. I struggled to focus on my speech as I held onto the wooden stand with all my strength. Just as I thought I would faint, I felt someone come up from behind me, help me regain my balance, and keep me standing upright. I looked behind me, and I discovered no one was there. I was being supported by an unknown source, and gratitude filled my soul! With this unseen help holding me up I was able to deliver the whole speech.

When I returned to my seat, Laurie leaned over and said, "I thought you were going to faint up there, but then you gained strength from nowhere!" With emotion in my voice, I filled her in on the unseen help.

Within days of the speech, I was readmitted to the hospital. Despite being sick, I remained full of gratitude for the unseen help. Once the news story aired, it brought about a greater awareness of children going hungry at school. This led to a nationwide online discussion, causing many New Zealanders to demand change.

The unseen help did not end there. I had a similar experience after a Feed the Need board strategy meeting. One of the board members, Jodi, had stayed behind to help me clean up after the meeting. Whilst I was washing the dishes in the kitchen sink, Jodi went to stack up the chairs. As soon as she left the room, I sensed a presence behind me. I quickly turned around to see a man standing in the kitchen doorway. He looked tangible, but I knew that he had passed on from this life, well before my time.

He was Māori, dressed in traditional clothing, and he held a tokotoko with Māori engravings, similar to the walking stick that Rawiri used. He looked at me as if he was gazing deep into my soul. I stood there in shock, looking back at him, wondering if he would say anything to me and why he was there. He then swiftly departed. Immediately, I telephoned Laurie to tell her about the experience. She gasped and told me that her dad, Rawiri, had experienced something similar at the board meeting. The following day, Rawiri and Laurie came to visit me. Rawiri explained that during the board meeting he had seen a number of Māori spirits surrounding us. Amongst those he described was the man I had seen. Rawiri said that the man was a Māori chief.

"Why did they come to our meeting?" I asked. "It is my feeling that they are ancestors of some of the children we serve and that they are supporting us in our efforts." Rawiri paused, then added, "Our ancestors remain ever present in our lives, often unseen."

I was, once again, left with a feeling of gratitude, but with many unanswered questions: Who supported me whilst I delivered that speech? Was it one of my ancestors or one of the ancestors of the children we were serving? And, as for those spirits who attended the board meeting, who were their descendants? I feel privileged to have had those experiences. I believe that we are not alone, that there are souls, even our ancestors, who are on the other side, supporting us in our trials and cheering us on in our worthy endeavours.

Chapter 18

Immeasurable Donations

"I'M SORRY IT'S NOT MUCH MONEY. I WISH I HAD MORE MONEY TO give you," twelve-year-old Mary-Jane said with regret in her tone.

Mary-Jane's father had emailed me a week earlier, asking if Mary-Jane could meet with me. He explained that she had dedicated her entire summer to baking and selling food to raise money to help Feed the Need. Here she was, apologising to me about it not being much money." On the contrary," I said with a lump in my throat. "Mary-Jane, imagine seeing forty children standing in front of you. That's a lot of children, right?"

She nodded. "These forty children usually go hungry at lunchtime, but because of you, they will receive a yummy, hot lunch. Do you think it will mean a lot to them?" She nodded, and then tears began to well up in her eyes as it dawned on her that her donation would make a real impact. She then gave me the biggest smile, no longer regretting the amount she'd raised but feeling rather pleased with what she had achieved.

Feed the Need received many donations over the years—some from large businesses, several from other charities, and many from individuals like Mary-Jane. Each donation has been a godsend, but some of the donors have stood out as people who exemplify what I believe, true giving is all about *sacrifice*. The dollar amount of their donations has not mattered as much as the immeasurable sacrifices they have made and the love they have shared.

Over the years, I have been privileged to learn about, meet, and connect with some of these individuals, and they have become my heroes. Without them knowing it, they have motivated and inspired me.

A Catholic school adopted Feed the Need as a charity for their students to focus on and gain hands-on experience while addressing a social issue. The students made planter boxes and started a vegetable garden so they could donate their harvest to Feed the Need. Some months later, they delivered their first harvest.

Each vegetable box was labelled "Grown with Love". I was moved by these sticky labels! But when I learned about Blake, the phrase "grown with love" took on a whole new meaning. Blake, a young student at the school, had cerebral palsy. This condition limited his mobility and caused him a lot of pain. Blake volunteered to water the vegetable garden every day, even on the weekends.

Blake's parents and teacher became concerned that it was too much for his little body. However, he insisted on doing the watering himself, without any assistance. His dedication to watering the garden was both touching and worrisome for every bystander, including his classmates, who saw him struggle with the weight of the watering cans. When people asked him why he did it, he replied that he wanted to "help the hungry children" and did not want his limitations to prevent him from serving those who were "less fortunate".

I cried for hours after learning about Blake. I repeatedly pictured this little boy's dedication, sacrifice, and desire to serve. The vegetables had indeed been "grown with love".

Blake became one of my biggest heroes. His example often gave me renewed energy for my calling to feed the children. I would often say to myself when my body felt too tired, "If little Blake can do it, so can I!"

I have seen many other inspiring examples of people who have helped in the cause to feed the need. Here are just a few:

A young mother who was battling cancer asked her extended family members to donate to Feed the Need instead of buying gifts for her daughter's first birthday. Traditionally, in her culture, it is believed that the more gifts a child receives on his or her first birthday, the more prosperous his or her life will be. This mother's illness had caused her to reflect on the meaning of life. If she lost the battle with cancer, what legacy would she leave for her daughter? This mother decided to break this cultural tradition in the hope that her daughter would grow up valuing compassion, selfless giving, and service over prosperity.

A man emailed me saying he had been inspired to do something good after learning about Feed the Need. He heard about a Mongolian hospital in need of an ambulance, so he raised funds to purchase one. He wasn't from Mongolia, but he cared about the plight of the hospital. He used all his savings, left his job, and drove all the way across a continent to deliver the much-needed ambulance.

The biological grandparents of our adopted daughter had some savings set aside. They generously donated their savings to our food programme to ensure we could feed as many children as possible. I still marvel at how special this donation was! I received an email from a man called "Joe," offering to help Feed the Need. I asked him what skills he had to offer. "I am 93 years old and confined to my bed, but I have a willing heart and want to help." I was immediately touched by his eagerness to help despite his limitations. Joe came up with some excellent suggestions of how he could help while confined to his bed, such as writing letters to local council leaders asking the government to introduce a food-in-school programme. Joe taught me that whatever your age, whatever your ability, you still have something to offer this world.

An engaged couple, Lily and Dan, asked for their wedding guests to donate to Feed the Need rather than shower them with wedding gifts on their special day. The donation ended up being a significant amount of money which went straight to feeding the need.

A man who was inspired by my story decided to close his optician clinic for six months and go to Kenya to offer free service to those who could not afford to see an optician.

A reserved and shy man wanted to do something to help. He was sensitive to the needs of others, and, like me, had lost sleep thinking about those going without. It took him weeks to pluck up the courage to speak to the CEO of the company he worked for, as he had an idea of how the company could help. The company ended up donating and distributing supplies to the families we served.

Upon learning about Feed the Need and its cause, a man walked into one of the schools we served and gave them $1,000 to be used to help any children going without. He wanted to remain anonymous. These were just a few of many immeasurable donations that came from all walks of life—from different cultures, backgrounds, religions, ages, and races. These donors had one thing in common: they were all examples of charity in action. These individuals recognised that we are all connected, that everyone is part of the human family, and that we should take care of each other.

Chapter 19

More Compassion, Less Judgement

John was a well-known and respected television presenter in New Zealand. He asked to meet me, to learn more about Feed the Need. As we sat down to chat, his genuine, kind, and warm personality came through.

As John and I discussed food insecurity in New Zealand, I found it hard to contain my emotions. I had met many children who struggled with hunger and their struggles weighed heavily on my mind. The reality was that Feed the Need and other charities were working hard to alleviate hunger, but our efforts were not enough. We needed the government to understand the gravity of the situation so something could be done to address this issue.

John asked me if there were any parents and children at the schools we served who might be willing to be interviewed. Debbie, a young mother of six children, courageously agreed to be interviewed.

On the day of the interview, Debbie was understandably very nervous. It was not easy for her to admit that she was struggling to feed her family, especially in front of a whole nation.

"What do you say to those people watching who say, 'It is the parent's responsibility to feed their children'?"

"It *is* our responsibility," Debbie acknowledged. "Yes, at the end of the day, it is, but just a little extra help from anywhere would be great."

During the interview, the reporter asked Debbie for permission to look inside her refrigerator. The fridge was empty except for a few carrots and half-used condiments.

Debbie admitted that she worried every week about not having enough food for her children. She added that she often went without food to ensure that her children had something to eat. This reminded me of my grandmother, who struggled to put food on the table. It made me wonder how many times my grandmother, like Debbie, went without food to ensure that her children had something.

In the hours that followed the interview being aired on national television, some viewers wrote harsh comments online.

"That mother doesn't deserve those kids."

"She was wearing a fashionable jumper; why is she able to afford that but not feed her kids?"

"She's a disgrace as a mother."

To me, Debbie was courageous for sharing her story with the nation. She genuinely hoped that by being honest about her struggle that she might bring about an awareness of other families who faced the same struggles. Thankfully, I can say that good things came from that interview. It began a nationwide discussion about food insecurity, particularly children going hungry at school. Politicians and business leaders watched the segment and made it their business to bring about change. I learned a lot about the negative aspects of human nature just from reading the comments about Debbie. For example, I learned that for some people, it's easier to tear others down than build them up. I learned how eager some people are to fill in the blanks of someone's life after seeing only a small glimpse. Some people even look for justification for why they won't help. They tell themselves, "I did it; why can't they?" or "They don't deserve my help". The reality is that we are not all dealt the same cards in life. How can we fully understand those less fortunate when we haven't walked in their shoes?

Other online comments and emails were directed to me, which said things like, "I have heard it's trendy for rich, bored, white women to set up charities." At the time, our finances were a big burden on my shoulders, I was not bored—I had children to raise. But it was not worth responding to those critics. They did not know me; they did not know my story. They said things like, "Go back to England. We don't want you." or "The food you are offering looks nasty." I chose not to respond.

There was one comment that I received, many times over, to which I wished I had responded. "You are enabling them. They need to be self-sufficient." Self-sufficiency is the ideal, but the reality was that these children were dependent on parents or caregivers, who, for various reasons, were not meeting their basic needs. Do you just let the children go hungry? No. That would not be fair nor right. I viewed our free lunches as something that would help these children concentrate at school and, hopefully, become self-sufficient one day, as my dad had done. As for the parents . . . I met many who were trying their best. Some had had difficult childhoods and were broken themselves. They had no positive footprint to follow. Others were working two or three low-paying jobs and still struggling to provide for their families. There were cases of severe illness or injury causing parents to lose everything they had worked for.

I repeat: The reality is that we are not all dealt the same cards in life. How can we fully understand those less fortunate when we haven't walked in their shoes? Perhaps they need our compassion more than our judgement.

Chapter 20

Hope

"We should remove the word *hope* from our mission statement and website," advised a Feed the Need board member. "The word *hope*," she said, "has a religious connotation that might deter people from donating."

As the board discussed whether we should remove the word *hope*, my thoughts turned to my dreams and the hopelessness I had seen and felt. It was crystal clear to me that if we removed the word *hope*, we would be removing one of the charity's core purposes.

I shared this thought with the board, including the fact that at one of the schools we served, 43 percent of the students were in state care. This meant that almost half of the school had been neglected or abused by those who should have cared for them. The word *hope* wasn't something to be debated; we needed to bring hope with every meal we served. The board agreed that the word would remain in our mission statement.

Martin Luther King III once spoke about creating what he called a "beloved community". He wisely said, "It's about creating more of that precious commodity that we call hope—real hope—for the forgotten, disadvantaged, and marginalised citizens of our communities, regardless of their race."[6] So how do we create hope? We seek out and serve those who are downhearted, struggling, or impoverished. This not only meets their temporal needs but more importantly, it demonstrates that we care, which in turn makes them feel valued. What a powerful formula to create hope!

I once saw the impact of this precious commodity as a result of a plea from a community leader. "Please do something to help our troubled youth'," this leader said. Initially, I felt unable to help. I was not trained in this line of work. I wasn't a social worker, youth worker, counsellor, or therapist. Besides, my young family had expanded once again, and I now had five children to look after.

Our fifth child came after a difficult in vitro fertilisation treatment and challenging pregnancy. In addition to the demands of a new baby, my compromised health, and running Feed the Need and the café, I felt I had nothing to offer these youth. However, after I prayed about these young people, an idea entered my mind. Feed the Need could begin a youth engagement programme offering opportunities for youth to obtain food-handling certificates and gain work experience in our kitchen.

We soon partnered with a second-chance school and posted the job opening through them. In the post, we intentionally omitted any mention of payment or wage. Instead, we highlighted that workers would be "part of the solution in alleviating food insecurity for children at school." We were inundated with applications.

Most applicants had been kicked out of school due to behavioural issues and had been in trouble with the law. They couldn't find work, and many were homeless. Their prospects looked hopeless.

When they walked into our interviews, many seemed to have indifferent attitudes and a confident swagger. We discussed the job responsibilities: getting up early in the morning, cooking, serving lunches, and cleaning up. Astonishingly, not one applicant asked if this job was paid. Instead, their questions focused on food insecurity,

---

6. Martin Luther King III, in Jenna Knaupp, "Forum: The beloved community," Sept. 28, 2021, news.byu.edu/intellect/forum-elements-of-a-beloved-community.

many sharing their own experiences of going hungry and expressing a strong desire to become part of the solution.

One young man initially seemed like a closed book. We asked him, "What can we do to help you get the most out of this work experience?"

"Can you help me improve my self-confidence?" he replied.

His answer revealed volumes. We concluded that these youths' stoic demeanours were a false bravado and a way of protecting themselves. As we continued to interview them, we were often given glimpses into what lay behind their facades. They were soft-hearted individuals who cared deeply. Within days of scheduling youth to join us in the kitchens, we received warnings from well-meaning people: These young women and men were unreliable. They won't work well in a team or accept any direction. Some of them are dangerous. I admit I had a few sleepless nights! However, as soon as our new helpers arrived in the kitchens, my concerns were instantly dispelled. Contrary to what we were told, they arrived on time, took direction well, worked hard, and were great team players. We had always intended to pay them, and when we asked for their bank account details, they all screamed and jumped with excitement.

Many of them had been abandoned or hurt as children, later rejected by society, and labelled as hopeless. Yet here they were, grasping this opportunity to make a difference. They rose to the challenge, knowing that we believed in them. They often commented that they had never felt so much love as they did in the Feed the Need kitchen.

Once when I was visiting one of the schools, I met up with Rikki, who managed and mentored the youth in our kitchen. Rikki had brought along a young man to help deliver the lunches that day. The young man was new to the programme, and this was my first time meeting him. I hugged Rikki and then hugged our new employee. As I did so, he whispered something in my ear. I did not understand his words, but I felt a shiver run down my spine. I knew it was not good.

That night, I had a dream in which I saw this same young man standing at a crossroads. One road was well-lit, and the other was dark. As I looked down these roads, I saw that the well-lit road offered a life of happiness, goodness, and hope and that the dark road offered a life of misery, crime, hate, and hopelessness. The young man chose to walk down the dark road. I woke up in a panic, with my heart racing. I felt I must tell Rikki about my dream. But it was only 3:00 a.m., so I decided to wait until later to text him.

As I lay in bed trying to go back to sleep, I felt uneasy and sensed that time was of the essence. I texted Rikki. I apologised for the early hour but said that it was urgent. I texted the details of my dream. Twenty minutes later, Rikki texted me back, saying that he had forgotten to set his phone to silent. Rikki thought that this young man might be involved in a gang and said that he would talk with him later that morning. I felt relief come over me, knowing that Rikki would help the young man. I then managed to get a few more hours of sleep.

At 2:00 p.m. that afternoon, I got a text from Laurie. She said, "I heard you've been dreaming again." She then phoned me and filled me in on what had transpired with the young man I had seen at the crossroads.

Laurie explained that she had received a phone call from the young man's second-chance school, saying that when he arrived at our work placement, we must terminate his employment. Apparently, he had been threatening and intimidating other students at his school, and the school was going to expel him. Laurie rang Rikki to pass on the instructions she had been given.

"No! No!" Rikki said. "Kerry texted me at 3:00 a.m. about this young man, as she had a dream about him. We can't let him leave our work placement. I need time to work with him so he doesn't go down the wrong path in life."

Laurie understood. After all, she had been raised by a father who dreamed a lot, and she believed in his dreams and mine. She phoned the school and said that Feed the Need needed to continue employing this young man.

When the young man arrived at our kitchen, Rikki pulled him aside and told him about the phone call from his school, but assured him that he could stay employed with Feed the Need. The young man was very appreciative and proceeded to tell Rikki about his involvement in a gang. He could not see a way out of his predicament, as the gang was the only "family" he had. Rikki assured him there was another way and offered to help him. The young man took Rikki up on his offer. He was still expelled from school, but he left his old life behind him and chose a new path.

In the Disney film *Moana*, there is a scene in which a volcano spits out hot lava at anyone who comes near. Moana knows that this angry volcano is actually a beautiful island called Te Fiti, but Te Fiti has forgotten who she is because her heart has been stolen. Moana has found Te Fiti's heart and intends to return it.

Moana bravely walks towards the raging volcano and tells her that although her heart has been stolen, this does not define her. She, Te Fiti, finally remembers who she really is. The volcano stops hurling hot lava and opens up, allowing Moana to place the heart back inside. The volcano then changes into a beautiful, lush, green, tranquil island full of trees and flowers.

I wept when I first saw this scene unfold. The raging volcano reminded me of some of the young men and women we had worked with, whose hearts had been "stolen" or broken. They prevented people from getting close to them. The opportunity to work in Feed the Need's kitchen—being treated as essential team players who were empowered, respected, appreciated, loved, and a part of something good—helped them realise their worth.

Everyone who watched these youths working hard in our kitchens stood back in awe, visibly touched. Celebrities, community leaders, business leaders, and volunteers from all walks of life became teary-eyed as they worked alongside them.

Years later, I learned that some of the youths, including the young man I had seen at the crossroads in my dream, had formed a charity to help others leave the gang lifestyle and start afresh. A young woman decided to volunteer weekly in a children's hospital, reading books to terminally ill children. The young man who had asked us to help with his confidence went on to attend a university.

So, this precious commodity that we call hope is something we must hold on to. I had aspired to give hope to hungry children. My hope was strengthened and expanded as I watched these youths in action—young women and men who had been mistreated, abused, and neglected yet still had the desire to do good and serve. I have learned that hope can exist in the most hopeless of situations. Can you imagine the positive ripple effect hope can have, not just in our own lives but in our communities and, dare I say, even throughout our global family?

Chapter 21

Facing Opposition

"We do not know of a single child who is going without lunch at any of our schools," said a community leader at a meeting I attended.

His statement stunned me. Was he in denial? Was he trying to cover up the truth, or had he simply never spoken to any school principals, teachers, or children in his community? Giving this man the benefit of the doubt, I explained to him and the other community leaders that, unfortunately, a significant number of children were going hungry at school. Some teachers were even making extra sandwiches at home to make sure their students did not go hungry.

Feed the Need was serving a number of schools within this community, so I organised this meeting in the hope of building positive relationships with community leaders. Yet they clearly did not welcome me. They met me with intimidating stares and angry body language. I was clueless about why, and I tried to dismiss the feeling in the room.

Most people in the room sat down, but one community leader remained standing. She pointed her finger at me and, with an aggressive tone, said, "Listen! Our community does not need people like you! I suggest you go back to the north shore or wherever you come from and stay there. You are not welcome. Your charity is not wanted or needed here."

My body began to shake. This hostility was unexpected and intimidating.

The phrase "people like you" repeated over and over in my mind. What did she mean? She didn't even know me. This was the first time we had ever met. Was it because I wasn't a New Zealander? Or because I lived on the north shore? Did she not want her community to accept charity from outsiders?

Fortunately, I was not alone in this meeting. Jodi, a Feed the Need board member, was with me. I had noticed, though, that when she had entered the room, she had been welcomed with open arms and a peck on the cheek, even though the community leaders had just met her.

I realised that this hostility was not about whether the children were going hungry or not. For some reason, their issue was with me.

I have always had an aversion to confrontation. As this group continued to intimidate me, I thought it best to get up and leave. As I was about to stand up, an image flashed through my mind. I saw the boy who had held my face. Then many other children's faces came to my mind, reminding me that I had a calling to fulfil. I felt a surge of protectiveness and courage come over me, and I remained seated.

I felt frustrated that these leaders, who were supposed to represent the people in their community, were willing to let children go hungry rather than acknowledge their needs and accept help. With my body trembling, I said, "Whether you acknowledge it or not, there *are* children going hungry in your community. Whether you welcome me or not, I *will* continue to serve the children in this area."

At this point, Jodi stepped in and told the community leaders how much heart and soul I had put into this, even mentioning some of the personal sacrifices I had made. As she spoke, most of the community leaders softened towards me, even offering to help. However, some continued to stare at me coldly.

Although this meeting did not go as planned, it taught me one important lesson: we may seek to be understood and want to be accepted or even liked, but not everyone will understand us or like us, and that's okay.

We will all face opposition from time to time. When this happens, my natural response is to walk away. However, when the opposition is against *my family* and *my calling,* I am able to dig deep and stand firm.

Nothing could have prepared me, though, for my next meeting with one of New Zealand's wealthiest businessmen. This man was known for his generous giving to various charities. Because of this, I had assumed he was compassionate and caring.

Within seconds of meeting him, he made it clear that he wanted this meeting to be over and done with. He threw many questions my way without allowing me to answer. When I did manage to reply, he became irritated. Two of his staff members also sat in on the meeting. Whenever they tried to speak or intervene, he shut them down too.

I will never forget how he spoke about people who relied on the welfare system as "being lazy, useless, drug users, and a burden on society".

I thought about the many parents who were working two or three jobs, trying to make ends meet. I thought of my grandmother resorting to cooking fat to relieve her children's hunger. No one chooses these conditions. Had he no compassion? I felt as if I were a Dickens character asking Scrooge for a donation and hearing, "Are there no prisons? And the Union workhouses? Are they still in operation?"[7] I thought it ironic that this man was known for his philanthropy. The reality was that his giving did not come from a place of compassion, empathy, or understanding. I shuddered to think how the recipients of his *charitable* donations would feel if they knew how harshly he judged them.

Hoping to change his opinion, I explained that my dad grew up relying on the welfare system and that my grandparents were not lazy, useless, or drug users. He rolled his eyes, leaned forwards, and said, "Well, obviously, your grandparents didn't work hard enough, then!"

---

7. Charles Dickens, *A Christmas Carol in Prose; The Chimes; The Cricket on the Hearth* (1846), 16.

I felt a lump form in my throat and said a silent prayer that I may be able to keep myself composed. I plucked up the courage to keep going and explained that my dad, as a child, had benefited greatly from the government-assisted lunch programme in England, adding that he was able to concentrate in class after his school lunches and went on to have a successful career.

He leaned towards me again, this time with a smirk on his face, and said, "Ha! If kids go hungry, it builds character. Your dad's story just proved that! Your dad became successful because of his hardship."

At this point, one of his staff tried to intervene, only to be shut down again. The businessman then asked me if I had any children of my own, and I nodded. He asked, "How many children do you have, and what are their ages?"

As I replied, he sat back in his chair, seemingly amused with himself. Then pointed his finger at me and said, "You, my dear, are neglecting and failing your own family by wasting your time on this worthless charity work. Those you serve will not remember you or appreciate your efforts. But your own children will remember your neglect!"

His words cut me to the core, and tears welled up in my eyes. The businessman had a gleeful expression on his face. He was obviously satisfied that he had made me tearful.

He then proceeded to take out his chequebook and asked, "Okay, so you came here for money, didn't you?"

I could not utter a word.

In a frustrated tone, he said, "Come on! Let's get to the point. How much were you after?"

I shook my head and quietly said that I wasn't sure anymore. He assumed I wasn't sure about the dollar figure, so he prodded me for an amount.

That wasn't it. Feed the Need definitely needed the money. I hesitated because I knew that if I accepted his cheque, he would visit the schools, as all sponsors did. He would meet the children and some of the parents. Knowing how he felt about them, I feared he would strip them of their *mana* (dignity) and try to shame them. Once again, I felt a surge of protectiveness for those I served and for their families. I could not allow this man to belittle or shame any child or parent, even though we needed his money.

"I did come here looking for funding, but the arrangement would not work with you."

"You have wasted my time!" he snapped.

As he stood up and walked towards the door, one of the other men approached him and whispered something in his ear. This caused the businessman to turn around and face me." I have been blunt and spoken harshly, but I am not the only one who thinks this way. I think you deserve to hear the truth. Believe me when I say that you're wasting your time. Those you serve are a thankless bunch, and your efforts are in vain. Would you prefer me to lie or tell the truth?"

Feeling fragile, I simply replied, "The truth."

He nodded and said, "I thought you would."

As we left the room, the man who had tried to intervene during the meeting offered to walk me down the stairs. I politely refused, as I did not want him to witness my inevitable flood of tears, which had been building up inside. However, he insisted. When we reached the stairwell, I began sobbing uncontrollably, and my cries echoed loudly throughout the concrete stairwell.

The man nodded as if to say, "Let it all out. I understand."

He put his hand on my shoulder and asked, "Who sent you into this lion's den?"

I could not reply, so he offered me a hug, which I accepted. A hug was exactly what I needed! After I had composed myself a little, he looked into my eyes and said, "Today I did not see a mother neglecting her family, but rather a mother who was being an example to her family." He continued, "During that meeting, I felt the love you have for those children you serve. That is a beautiful thing. I want you to picture one of the children you have served. Can you do that for me?"

I nodded.

'This child knows you love him," he said, "and because of that, the work you do is worth your time and effort. Don't be discouraged by today's meeting. Hold on to your worthy cause."

His words brought me great comfort. We hugged again and said our goodbyes.

"Lion's den" was an accurate description! The businessman had attempted to swallow me whole with his cynical, critical, and harsh words. His attacks did hurt, and I was disheartened that anyone could think that way about those less fortunate. Perhaps, I thought, it's people like this businessman who give charity a bad name by stripping others of their dignity and self-worth.

Looking back at my meeting with the community leaders, I can understand if they questioned my intent, thinking that I might have shared the same sentiments as this businessman. Yet my intent was always to protect, serve, and love the children in their community, never to shame them. Never.

The businessman's attacks on me as a mother and on my charitable efforts left some scars. In fact, I might have given up on Feed the Need that day if I had not had my dreams and impressions to lean on.

Shortly after that meeting, I was able to get the needed funding from another philanthropist—a person with a good heart and pure intent.

We are all bound to meet cynics now and again whose intention is to tear us down, but we must not let them extinguish our hope, vision, light, or good works.

Chapter 22

A Challenge to Prove That God Is Real

One of Feed the Need's greatest supporters, whom I will call Martin, once asked me, "Kerry, do you believe in God? Do you believe in life after death?"

"I do," I replied.

He then told me he was an atheist and playfully challenged me to prove God was real. Martin was a very intellectual man and a high-profile leader, so I wondered how I could *prove* to him that God was real.

I decided to tell him about my dreams, the *real* reason behind Feed the Need. This intrigued him. He asked if I had any other experiences I could share. I ended up telling him about an experience I had with a teenage girl in trouble.

One night, my sleep was disturbed by somebody standing next to the bed. Initially, I thought it was one of the kids, but I quickly realised that, once again, I was receiving a visit from a soul who had passed on. I closed my eyes and prayed for that being to leave, but then a calm feeling came over me.

This soul was the deceased father of a teenager I knew, although I did not know her very well. He told me that his daughter was planning to take her life. He explained, in detail, the reasons she had come to that decision. By the time he finished, I was moved to tears, realising how much this girl had been through!

The father asked me to tell his daughter about his visit, including all the details that no one else knew, and to hug her and tell her he loved her. I promised I would, and then he was gone.

The next morning, I became nervous. I did not doubt the visit, but I did doubt my own ability to be the messenger. Later that day, I invited the girl to go to town with me. On the drive there, she seemed happy. She openly shared her hopes of travelling the world, teaching English in foreign lands, and singing on stage. I was confused, and I decided not to say a word about her father's visit.

On the way back to her house, I felt as though someone gently pushed me. I knew at that moment that it was her father, giving me the nudge I needed. I blurted out about her father's visit, and she stared at me in disbelief. When I pulled into her driveway, I recounted everything her father had told me, in detail. She burst into tears and turned away from me, occasionally turning back at me, exclaiming, "No one knows any of those things!"

After some time, she reached over and hugged me tightly, crying. She then sat back in her seat, letting out a huge sigh. "I know that my dad visited you because no one knows any of those things."

There is much more to this story which I am not at liberty to disclose, but I am happy to report that the father's visit was life-changing for his daughter. She did go on to travel the world and teach English in foreign lands.

After I recounted this story to Martin, he became subdued. He didn't offer up any theories about the experience. He just sat there deep in thought and then said, "Kerry, it is clear to me that your life has purpose and that you sincerely believe you were called to do charity work. So, I am curious, what do you think *my* calling is?"

I thought for a moment and replied, "I believe your life's calling is to be a leader, as this comes naturally to you. I also believe that this calling comes with a responsibility, to be a *righteous* leader."

Martin nodded and began to tear up. "If there is a God, he won't love me. I'm not a very good person."

I assured him that God loved him.

"If you are right about God," he said in a hushed tone, "then I need to make some changes in my life. You have given me a lot to think about. Thank you."

As we parted ways that day, it seemed that Martin was questioning his atheism. Even better, he was considering a new reality: that our lives have purpose, that life goes on after death, that our earthly relationships continue after death, and that there is a God who knows us.

I was relieved that Martin knew the real reason behind Feed the Need. He continued to remain a great supporter of the cause.

Chapter 23

Eyes That See

"In school, we were not allowed to speak our own language," Hararei, a family friend, told me with downcast eyes. Recollecting his childhood experiences all those years ago seemed upsetting for him, but he continued, "We had to speak English only. If the teachers overheard us talking to each other in Te Reo Māori, or if we replied in class in Te Reo Māori, we would have our hands and knuckles beaten with the edge of a ruler and our backsides hit hard with the cane."

As I listened to Hararei, I found myself gasping time and time again in utter shock. I wasn't reading this in an old history book. I was actually speaking with someone who had experienced it firsthand.

Hararei and his family extended the hand of friendship to our family shortly after we moved to New Zealand. They were warm, friendly, kind and treated us like family. There was nothing to suggest that Hararei had experienced such harsh treatment in an effort to make him more British. Here he was, welcoming a British family into his home. He didn't open up about experiencing racial discrimination until years later when I asked him about it. This wasn't the first or the last time I heard stories such as these that demonstrated the inequitable and unjust treatment of the Māori people.

Dame Whina Cooper, on whom the title "Mother of the Nation" has been bestowed, tirelessly advocated for her people throughout her life. She spoke out boldly against the unjust treatment of the Māori, leading to notably diminished racial discrimination in health care, employment, land ownership, and housing. At age 79, she led a peaceful protest highlighting the ongoing loss of Māori land, walking almost 700 miles. By the time she arrived at Parliament, she had an estimated 5,000 people behind her in support and 60,000 signatures demanding the return of Māori land.[8]

As a result of Whina Cooper's march, the New Zealand Parliament enacted the Treaty of Waitangi Act to resolve grievances relating to Māori land. By August 2018, settlements had reached a value of $2.24 billion.[9]

"I've been waiting for years for men to put the world to rights. And they hadn't. Well, God gave me eyes to see, a head to think, a tongue to talk. Why not use them, why not share what I know?" Whina said.[10]

Without courageous and committed people like Whina, the injustices and inequality in New Zealand might be prevalent today. As Dr. Martin Luther King Jr. said, "History is the long and tragic story of the fact that privileged groups seldom give up their privileges voluntarily."[11] It was necessary for people like Whina to stand up and demand change.

---

8. See "Cooper, Whina (1895–1994)", encyclopedia.com; "Celebrating Dame Whina Cooper and the fight for Māori land rights", New Zealand Parliament website, https://www.parliament.nz/en/get-involved/features/celebrating-dame-whina-cooper-and-the-fight-for-maori-land-rights/.

9. See "Celebrating Dame Whina Cooper and the fight for Māori land rights", New Zealand Parliament website, https://www.parliament.nz/en/get-involved/features/celebrating-dame-whina-cooper-and-the-fight-for-maori-land-rights/.

10. Whina Cooper, in Michael King, *Whina: A Biography of Whina Cooper* (Auckland: Hodder and Stoughton, 1983), 180.

11. Martin Luther King Jr., "Letter from Birmingham Jail", in *A Testament of Hope: The Essential Writings and Speeches of Martin Luther King Jr.*, ed James Melvin Washington (1986), 292.

On December 1, 1955, an African American woman, Rosa Parks, boarded a city bus. During this time of segregation in the United States, white people were allocated seating towards the front of the bus, while Black people were expected to sit in the back. In New Zealand, from 1925 to the early 1960s, similar segregation existed. On buses travelling to Auckland, Māori were forced to give up their seats to white passengers if the buses became full.

Rosa Parks sat in a seat directly behind the portion allocated for white people. When the bus driver saw that a white man didn't have a seat, he instructed four Black people, including Rosa Parks, to give up their seats directly behind the white section. The other three left their seats, but Rosa quietly refused.

Rosa was subsequently arrested and prosecuted, but her courage was not for naught. She began a movement that influenced change through a quiet act of defiance.[12] Rosa Parks is often referred to as the "Mother of the Civil Rights Movement."

Whina and Rosa's stories are strikingly similar. Both have been given the title of "Mother"—one of a nation, the other of a movement. Later, Rosa stated, "When I made that decision, I knew I had the strength of God and my ancestors with me."[13] I expect that Whina, like Rosa, also felt the strength of her ancestors as she walked those 700 miles to "put the world to rights". Just as Rosa and Whina drew strength from their ancestors to confront injustice on a public stage, I saw quiet courage in my own home—in the way my Irish mother endured the subtle, everyday indignities of prejudice.

As a child, I witnessed my mother being ridiculed in the form of "Irish jokes." These jokes stereotyped and labelled the Irish as drunks, angry and incapable. Although people thought these jokes were harmless, I saw firsthand the hurt they caused my mother as people laughed at her expense.

I feel that the more people educate themselves about those who are different from us, the more likely they will dispel long-held false assumptions and views. During my years with Feed the Need, I learned

12. See Rosa Parks with Jim Haskins, *My Story* (1992), 113–34.

13. Rosa Parks with Gregory J. Reed, *Dear Mrs. Parks: A Dialogue with Today's Youth* (1996), 42.

that despite my good intentions, I sometimes excluded others by being culturally insensitive.

Whilst visiting the schools one day, I noticed a child sitting at a table without any lunch in front of him. He was awkwardly twiddling his fingers, trying not to be noticed. I could not take my eyes off him and eventually asked the teacher why the boy was not eating our lunches along with everyone else." He is Muslim and only eats halal meat," she said, "but he does enjoy your vegetarian soups when you occasionally provide them." My heart sank. For four years, I had unintentionally excluded this boy from our lunch programme, purely because I hadn't given any thought to students with religious dietary requirements.

It dawned on me that the boy represented other children who could not participate in our lunch programme. I quickly approached the boy and apologised. I made him a promise that in the next few days Feed the Need would always provide an authentic vegetarian option so that he would never feel left out again. He was visibly pleased.

Was it a coincidence that the following day I met Ashia, who became instrumental in planning these authentic vegetarian dishes? Ashia and I met in the most unlikely of places: the emergency room. I was there because my son had hurt his arm and Ashia was working as a nurse.

As Ashia and I talked, she told me about her Indian heritage, her Muslim faith, and her love of cooking. In fact, she was in the middle of writing her first (of many) cookbooks with authentic Indian dishes. That's when I knew our meeting was not a coincidence. I told her about Feed the Need and my promise to the Muslim boy. Tears came to Ashia's eyes as she thought about this boy, and she volunteered her time to work on recipes for us to use. Sometimes people need to physically see things to realise how they might exclude others unintentionally. Proximity, along with seeking to understand, can help identify needs that might have previously gone unnoticed.

Another example of how I had been culturally insensitive involved Rawiri, the Māori man who had shared the same dream as me. Rawiri had first introduced himself to me as David. Throughout all the years we had served together, that was what I called him. However, I noticed when people spoke to him in Te Reo Māori, they called him Rawiri.

I later learned that many Māori people used the English versions of their names when they introduced themselves to Pakeha (white people). This made it easier for Pakeha to spell, remember, and pronounce their names.

I couldn't imagine having to change my name to accommodate the needs of others. I had been oblivious for so many years that I had been calling him the English version of his name rather than his name in his native tongue. Partway through writing this book, Rawiri sadly passed away. Shortly after his passing, I was given the impression to change his name from David to Rawiri in this book. Each time I made that change, I felt assured that Rawiri appreciated it.

It's encouraging to see that today, the indigenous language, Te Reo Māori, is being incorporated into many New Zealand schools. This rising generation of Māori children can openly embrace their language and culture, giving them a stronger sense of identity.

These experiences taught me to ask myself questions about cultures, people, religious practices, and so forth—questions like, "What don't I know?" and "What don't I understand?" I have learned that when I open my eyes and seek to understand, I can help others know they belong.

Chapter 24

Anxious to Do More Good

IN THE SOUTH ISLAND OF NEW ZEALAND IS A QUAINT TOWN CALLED Queenstown. Standing proud, next to its lake, is a monument that reads "SERVICE ABOVE SELF". It recognises those who lost their lives in the First and Second World Wars.

As I read the names listed on the monument, I found it remarkable that people in this small, picturesque town of New Zealand had signed up to fight a war that was far from home. There had been no bombs, air raids, sirens, or extermination camps on their doorstep—just serene lakes, breathtaking scenery, and sheep farms. It made me wonder if I, like those individuals listed on the monument, practise "service above self"? Am I willing to sacrifice for other people? Even people I don't know?

My great-grandfather "George William Robinson" served in the "Royal Navy Volunteer Reserve" regiment in World War I. In February of 1918, whilst aboard the SS Huntsmoor ship, a torpedo struck and sank the ship and sadly, my great-grandfather was killed. He was only twenty-eight years old, leaving behind his young pregnant wife, who bore a son—my grandfather—and named him George Robinson. When my grandfather grew up, he served in World War II and thankfully survived. My grandfather had eleven children, forty grandchildren, and over 150 great-grandchildren. George William Robinson, the young able seaman, who died all those years ago at only twenty-eight years old, could not have possibly imagined the legacy he left.

I was not called to fight a war, but I was called to serve. As a member of his posterity, I hope to use my time on earth wisely and make him proud.

So many people, like my great-grandad, have sacrificed their lives so that we can have freedom today, but what do we do with our freedom? What do we sacrifice for others? What do we do with our time?

One night, whilst sleeping, I became aware that someone was trying to wake me up. Upon waking, I could see that it was neither my husband nor my children, as they were all sound asleep. When I lay back down, I felt the presence of a recently departed soul.

Despite my belief in life after death, I swiftly put the bedcovers over my head and asked this soul to leave. Despite having had similar experiences like these before, I was still unnerved. But she was not deterred, and she stated her name. I instantly realised that she was the mother and grandmother of some friends of mine. I had never met or conversed with her in person, but I knew her name was June.

June explained that she had passed away just minutes earlier. It was very early in the morning, and I wondered if her family members were even aware of her passing. June continued speaking to me, saying she was happy. I was pleased for her, but perplexed about why she had come to tell this to me. I was not a relative or someone she knew.

In a hasty and bold manner, June said, "There is much work to do!"

What did she mean? I thought. *What work was she talking about?* But before I could ask her, she was gone! Only then did I pull the covers off my head and sit up straight in bed. I had many questions and thoughts running through my mind. Foremost was whether her family knew of her passing yet. Should I text or call them at this early hour? In my mind, I debated back and forth about whether I should tell her family about the visit at all. If I did, how would they take it?

I decided to sleep on it, but after much tossing and turning, I sat up again and sent a text to Kathy, one of June's daughters. I didn't mention her mother's visit or her passing but rather offered my love and support at this difficult time.

Around 7 a.m., whilst telling my husband about June's visit, I received a text from Kathy. Kathy had just been notified of her mother's passing and learned that her mother had passed away in the early hours of the morning. Kathy then read my text and noticed that the timing of my text coincided with the time of her mother's passing. The fact that I was offering love and support caused her to conclude that I must have had an experience with her mother. This was the perfect segue for me to share the details of her mother's brief visit. A few days later, Kathy and her grown-up children came and visited me. They thanked me for sharing my experience and relayed to me that June often told them that "there is much work to do" when they visited her. The family marvelled that after her passing, she had come to someone she hadn't known and repeated those same words.

Kathy then said she wondered what her mother meant by it. I too had been left speculating! After much thought, I came to the opinion that our lives pass quickly and that we must use our time to seek out and serve people in need, to go beyond our neighbourhoods and social circles, to serve others even when it's inconvenient. Be a voice for those who don't have one, protect those who are vulnerable, and be generous with our time and our means. We should be anxious to do more good.

I think of my brother David, who volunteered to serve in an orphanage in Kenya. The children instantly gravitated to his warm, friendly, caring, and kind disposition. The time he spent with the children was filled with singing, games, and laughter. When the time came for him to leave, the children were devastated. One child even embraced him around the neck, holding on with all his strength whilst sobbing uncontrollably. "It was the hardest goodbye," David said.

David was *anxious to do more* for those children. After giving it much thought, he came up with an idea. As these children did not have any pillows to lay their heads on at night, he decided to buy pillows and hand-sew the message, "I am a child of God," on each pillowcase. David hoped that each time they laid their heads on their pillows, they would feel loved, known, and of great worth. He is a great example to me.

I remember a time when a young mother of children in our lunch programme phoned me and asked if I had a spare coat for her three-year-old daughter. With it being winter, I hastily ran upstairs to my daughter's wardrobe and discovered we had not one but two spare coats. This led me to wonder if we had more surplus winter clothing in our home that we could give to this same family.

By the time my husband came home from work, our entrance hall was piled high with items from around the home. Curious and a little concerned, he asked, "What is going on?"

I told him about the mother's request for a coat. My husband pointed out the duvets, blankets, toys, food, and other items—much more than a single coat. I had to admit that once I began seeing all our surplus, I felt anxious to give it to this family. That evening my family and I packed up the car with these items. When we set off to make the delivery, Matt and the children were unenthused. The cold, wet, and dark evening only added to their grumbles.

Once we arrived, we began doing relays, taking items into this family's home. When the mother realised that we were delivering a whole lot more than a coat, she became tearful. Her children excitedly unboxed the toys and wrapped themselves in the blankets. Once we finished, she tearfully thanked us. She even stood in the rain and blew kisses to us as we drove away.

When she had faded out of sight, my husband pulled the car over to the side of the road. He took a deep breath, remained silent for a minute, and then tearfully said, "We could have given more! We could have done more. We should have done more!" Once he composed himself, we headed home. Our children were unusually quiet as we drove home. I believe they, too, had been moved by the experience.

I have learned that the experience of coming face-to-face with those in need changes us. It alters our focus and perspective, leaving us with a strong desire to do more and give more. We may not change the world, but we will change someone's world for the better.

I know this is true because my world has been changed by those who have loved and served me unconditionally. On one occasion, whilst I was very sick in the hospital and feeling overwhelmed, the nurse on duty came, stood by my bedside, held my hand, and shared some comforting words. She then proceeded to shower and dress me, as I had been too weak to do so. When she placed me back into bed, I felt calm, loved, and full of gratitude. Although the sickness remained relentless, I felt I could cope. I profusely thanked her and told her I loved her.

She took hold of my hand again and said, "My dear, I love you too." Some may say that she was just doing her job, but I know she did more than that. She changed the world for me during that difficult time.

People like my great-granddad, June, my brother, my husband, and my nurse have taught me to never tire of doing good. I hope to never leave this life saying, "I could have done more. I should have done more."

Chapter 25

God Knows Us by Name

BELONGING IS NOT JUST SOMETHING PEOPLE DESIRE. IT IS A NEED. WE come to earth wired to connect. Why? What's the purpose? My belief is that we all *belong* to the human family and that our lives are not by chance—that our need to connect and belong has a purpose and that there is a loving God who knows and loves each of us. This belief was reinforced through an experience I had involving a dream and a choir.

I found an opportunity for two youths to be sponsored to participate in a four-day camp in Utah in the United States. When we advertised this opportunity, many youths applied. Laurie and Rikki began interviewing these candidates. At the end of each day, our team wondered, "How will we decide on the final two?" Each one of them deserved the chance to go. Most of them had never left New Zealand.

One night after four days of interviews, I had a dream. I saw a young man with a long plait (braid) and then heard the name Jericho three times. When I woke up, I phoned Laurie asking if we would be interviewing anyone named Jericho that day, and told her about my dream. Laurie looked at her list of names and excitedly exclaimed that there was someone named Jericho scheduled for an interview that day! Jericho is an uncommon name in New Zealand. I had never met someone by that name.

As we entered the building where we would be conducting the interviews, Laurie took a quick peek into the room where the applicants were waiting. Then, with a big smile, she said, "There is a young man with a long plait in the waiting room!" We concluded that he must be Jericho! When the young man with the long plait walked into the room, I was in awe, as he was the same young man I had seen in my dream. I looked at Laurie and nodded to confirm he was the one.

However, there was a twist: his name was not Jericho; it was Joshua. So, who was Jericho? When it came time for Jericho's interview, a young woman walked in. We knew we had the two who were meant to go.

Later, Laurie informed Joshua and Jericho that they had been selected, and they were ecstatic. Neither had a passport, so Laurie helped them apply and organise the travel arrangements. Laurie would also accompany them on their travels and attend the four-day event.

My husband and I had family in Utah, so we decided to pay for our own trip there and spend a day with Laurie, Joshua, and Jericho before their event began. We gave Joshua and Jericho a list of tourist activities to choose from. Surprisingly, one of the things they chose was to attend a choir rehearsal in the city. It was a world-renowned choir called The Tabernacle Choir; because it was religious in nature, I had wrongly assumed that this might not appeal to them.

My husband and I planned to meet them at the choir rehearsal after they checked into their hotel. While we were waiting for them to arrive at the venue, my husband asked what their names were. "Joshua and Jericho." He then looked up something on his phone and said, "There's a song with both those names in its title. It's called 'Joshua Fit the Battle of Jericho.'"

Just moments later. The choir stood up and began to sing that same hymn, "Joshua fit the battle of Jericho!" Joshua, Jericho, and Laurie arrived as the choir was still singing the first verse. It didn't take them long to notice that this choir sang a hymn that included both of their names. They were thrilled.

Joshua commented that I must have arranged for the choir to sing this song for them. "No!" I told him. He gave me a look as if he didn't believe me. "Honestly, I couldn't have organised this even if I wanted to." I had no connections with this choir or its conductor.

Joshua and Jericho asked Laurie if she could take them to see the live broadcast a few days later. After the live broadcast had ended, the conductor spoke to the audience saying that the choir had been asked to sing the song "Joshua fit the battle at Jericho" again and implied that this was unusual. Joshua and Jericho turned to one another with the biggest smiles.

Two days later, while shopping in a store, Matt bumped into the very same choir conductor. Matt took this opportunity to tell him about my dreams, Joshua and Jericho, and the significance of The Tabernacle Choir performing "Joshua fit the battle at Jericho", not just once but twice in the live performance! The choir conductor was very excited to share this story with The Tabernacle Choir. I'm convinced that this experience—from the dream about Joshua and Jericho to the song which included both of their names, in a place far from home—was no coincidence. It powerfully added to my belief that we are all God's children and that He knows each of us by name.

Chapter 26

My Epiphany

An email marked "Highly Confidential" caught my attention in my inbox. I clicked on it, wondering what on earth this could be? A scam? But as the contents of the email presented themselves to me, I knew it was not. It was an email sent on behalf of Queen Elizabeth II. I had been nominated for a Royal Honour—namely, "The New Zealand Order of Merit"—for the contribution I had made "to New Zealand and its people".

I was invited to an "investiture ceremony" in which I would receive an insignia. The ceremony would be held in a New Zealand government building.

My jaw dropped. My heart raced. This couldn't be true!

It dawned on me that my dream about being in a government building all those years ago would be fulfilled, *literally*. You see, the months had turned to years, and my family and I had recently moved to Utah, in the United States. It seemed ever so unlikely that the third of my interconnected dreams would ever come to pass. Yet, something inside of me had held onto the *literal* fulfilment of this dream. After all, this was the same dream that Rawiri and I had dreamt when we were complete strangers. Surely it had to happen literally, right?

But I had never imagined that receiving a Royal Honour would be the reason for my being there. I had speculated that perhaps charities, including Feed the Need, would be invited to the government building to discuss solutions for food insecurity. It never crossed my mind that I would go there to receive an award.

Laurie had also been nominated for a Royal Honour for her involvement in Feed the Need, which meant that Rawiri, her father, who was still living at this point, would attend. Was it just a coincidence that Rawiri, who had been in the government building in my dream, was actually going to be there that day?

When the Royal Honours list was announced in the media, the news reached the birth family of our adopted daughter. They invited me to wear their family Korowai at the ceremony—the cloak of green and blue iridescent feathers. Knowing its significance in Māori culture, I felt that it might be frowned upon for a white English woman to wear a Korowai. Especially because it showcases the wearer's status, lineage, and connection to their ancestors and, these were not my ancestors. But when I prayed about it, I felt differently and accepted their beautiful gesture.

This feeling was confirmed when, before the ceremony, our adopted daughter's grandmother, Marion, placed the Korowai around my shoulders. The love, comfort, and support I felt in a tangible way will stay in my memory always.

The comfort of the Korowai stayed with me as the powerful invitation of the Māori call broke the silence, "Haere mai . . . haere mai ra"—

As I walked through the walnut-coloured wooden doors that I had seen in my dream years earlier, I saw Matt and other family members smiling proudly at me.

I saw Rawiri, who was holding his tokotoko, his ceremonial carved walking stick. He had opened a door for me in my dream, and as I walked down the red carpet, I was reminded once again that he had indeed opened many doors for me. Most important, he had opened the door to his people and his culture—a culture steeped in symbolism, traditions, and ancestral connections. Rawiri had unwavering belief in his dreams, a strong connection with his ancestors, a deep faith in God, and love, concern, and hope for his people. What a privilege it had been to serve with him. Ahead of me, I caught sight of Laurie at the end of the red carpet, wearing her family's Korowai. I wondered if she too had experienced a powerful feeling of love when her Korowai had been placed around her shoulders.

When we reached our seats, we, along with all the guests, were invited to be seated. The governor general welcomed us, and the announcer invited each recipient to stand when his or her name was called. When each person stood, the announcer gave a brief summary of that person's service to New Zealand.

When the announcer read my name, Kerry Louise Owen, my heart skipped a beat. This was my cue to stand. "Kerry Owen founded the charity Feed the Need . . . " The announcer briefed the guests about my work. I reflected on the dreams which had led me to this place. I found myself wondering about the brilliant bright light I had seen in that first dream, but my thoughts were interrupted when I was given the cue to walk up onto the stand.

The governor general engaged me in quiet conversation, instantly helping me feel at ease. As she pinned the insignia onto my blazer, she thanked me for my service and leaned forwards, saying, "New Zealand needs you home." Her use of the word *home* really struck a chord with me. *Home.* She was right, New Zealand was home! During the years I had lived there, it had indeed become home to my family and me. Was it because of its beautiful land and coast, which had instantly captivated me? Was it because our family had been blessed with three more children, including the daughter we had adopted from this land? Was it because the people of this land understood my dreams and that we shared the same spiritual language? Was it because the children in my dreams felt like my own family? Was it because of those I had served with and felt connected with? Yes. The answer to all these questions was an emphatic yes!

The governor general concluded the investiture ceremony with these remarks to the recipients, "Each of you has helped make New Zealand a better place. . . . Your actions and the stories we've heard reflect the spirit of the words of Mahatma Gandhi when he said, "The best way to find yourself is to lose yourself in the service of others."

"Your contributions have enriched the cultural, social, and economic fabric of Aotearoa, New Zealand. Please wear your insignia with pride.

"On behalf of the Queen of New Zealand and all New Zealanders, I congratulate you on your achievements, and I thank you for your service to our country."

We then stood and sang New Zealand's national anthem. Whilst singing, I was reminded of the first time I heard the anthem and how I was unexpectedly moved to tears. This time my tears flowed freely again.

I reflected on the brilliant bright light that I had seen beyond the doors in my dream but which I had *not* seen beyond the doors at this ceremony. In silent prayer, I asked, "What was the meaning of the light beyond the wooden doors in my dream?"

And then I had my epiphany: The brilliant, bright light was never about this building. It was never about this occasion.

It was all about love. God's love.

I finally understood! I had been invited on a journey to come closer to God—to walk in His light, His goodness, and His love. How fitting that this Korowai, which symbolised "the arms of love," had been placed around my shoulders prior to learning this final lesson. I had been taught about the real meaning of charity, the importance of hope, of having compassion for those in need, of serving unconditionally and to feel God's perfect love. Despite my imperfections and inadequacies, He believed in me and had allowed me to share that light, goodness, and love with those I served. My heart overflowed with joy and gratitude.

Chapter 27

Serving the One

The last time I saw Rawiri was the day of the investiture ceremony in May 2019. While there, Rawiri took the opportunity to tell guests and other recipients about our shared dream. Strangers approached me, wanting to hear more about my dreams but regretfully, I shied away. Rawiri embraced his spiritual gifts and boldly shared his experiences with others. He encouraged me to do the same, but I was a slow learner!

Had I known that day was the last time I would see Rawiri in person, I would have embraced him longer. I would have wept on his shoulder, thanked him profusely for his example, and told him I loved him. And, that I would never shy away from sharing my dreams again. In June 2021, Rawiri passed on from this life. I was left with a great sense of loss. It is not every day two strangers have the same dream. But, while writing this book, I felt Rawiri's presence several times, reaffirming that the souls of our departed loved ones are still with us.

One night, Rawiri visited me in a dream. He looked well and happy. All he said was, "*Tangata, tangata, tangata.*"

Upon waking, those words echoed in my mind and I was reminded of a declaration made by Meri Ngaroto, a Māori female chief, in the early nineteenth century.

She said:

Hutia te rito o te harakeke
Kei whea te kōrimako e kō?
Ki mai koe ki au
He aha te mea nui i te ao?
Maku e ki atu,
He tangata, He tangata, He tangata.

If the heart of the harakeke was removed,
Where would the bellbird sing?
If I was asked what was the most important thing
in the world
I would be compelled to reply,
It is people, it is people, it is people.

In my dream, Rawiri had said, "tangata, tangata, tangata," or "People, people, people." I thought I had already understood Ngaroto's sentiment—that people are the most important thing in the world. But after my dream, I was left wondering what Rawiri was trying to tell me. Was I missing something from Ngaroto's declaration?

Over the next few days, I learned that the harakeke (flax bush) is often used by Māori as a metaphor to describe the family. The centre shoots, the heart of the harakeke, represent those who are living and their future descendants. The outer edges represent their ancestors. All shoots being interconnected. If the heart of the harakeke is removed the whole plant dies. This understanding gave me a new perspective on serving, protecting, and nurturing *the one*—the living—the heart of the harakeke. When we serve the one, we are also serving their family: their living relations, their future descendants and even preserving the legacy of their ancestors.

It is in the "heart" of these interconnected shoots that the bellbird finds the ideal spot to sing its beautiful song. The harakeke is its safe haven. And so, if the plant dies, where would the bellbird sing?

I believe that Ngaroto, back in the early nineteenth century, fully understood the vital role bellbirds play in dispersing seeds, which aid forest regeneration in New Zealand. In protecting the heart of the harakeke, the bellbirds can continue this important role. Ngaroto illustrated the bigger picture of how *serving the one*, the heart of the harakeke, ultimately has a ripple effect on society as a whole.

Rawiri was emphasising the importance of *serving the one* and highlighting the fact that how we treat the *one* can impact generations. So, every time I am out *serving the one*, I am reminded of the bigger picture. To the *ones* . . ..

To the children—the heart of the harakeke—I want you to know that God knew you before I did. I was shown your beautiful faces and given a glimpse into the infinite love God has for you. To meet you in person, to embrace you, and to serve you, was the privilege of a lifetime. You are loved!

To the child who wrote to me saying, "Please don't forget me, please don't forget me, please don't forget me," I will never forget you, I will never forget you, I will never forget you! You taught me the importance of using every opportunity to tell those I serve that they are loved. I will never forget you or any of the children. Your faces are forever etched into my mind and heart. You are loved!

To the child who held my face and asked me, "Are you an angel?" I would still say no, but would add that I have been helped by angels on both sides of the veil and that it was God who blessed me with dreams so that I could find you. You are loved! To my own children: Thank you for sharing mummy with those in need. I have always felt privileged to be your mother, and I love you the "mostest".

To the angels who helped me, on this side of the veil, you know who you are. Thank you, you are loved!

Until my final breath, I will continue to follow my dreams. And when my life comes to a close, I look forward to reuniting with loved ones on the other side of the veil, including the angels who held me up when I was too weak to stand. And, to hear the beautiful bellbird sing forevermore, as it perches happily in the heart of the harakeke.

Hutia te rito o te harakeke
Kei whea to komako e ko?
Ki mai Ki ahau

He aha te mea nui i te Ao?
Maku e ki atu,
He tangata, he tangata, he tangata.

What Happened Next?

Before my family and I moved to America, I met up with Jacinda Ardern, the soon-to-be prime minister, over a mint tea. We talked about food insecurity and possible solutions. Jacinda promised that she would continue advocating for food in schools in Parliament. Soon after she was elected as prime minister, she announced a free school lunch programme. She kept her promise!

Laurie became the lead nutrition adviser for the Ministry of Education's "Healthy School Lunch Programme". She can look back and see how serving on the ground with Feed the Need prepared her for the work she does today.

Rawiri passed on from this world, but his legacy remains strong.

Feed the Need continues to alleviate food insecurity by providing food packs for school students to take home. I am still involved with the organisation's work and mission, and it will always have a special place in my heart. I am grateful to those people who now lead Feed the Need and volunteer their time to continue "feeding hope, one action at a time" (feedtheneed.co.nz).

Soon after moving to America, I accepted an invitation to become the Director of a new non-profit charity called Reach Out Today in an unpaid role. This charity alleviates needs within Utah, by providing hygiene packs, food packs, clothing, furniture, shopathons (helping clothe children living in poverty), pop-up hair salons (providing hair cuts to under-privileged children), and more!

I have continued to receive dreams, but I will leave those stories for another time. In the light of hindsight, I see those dreams as a blessing from the Divine. The gift of charity, which flowed toward those I served, also found its way back to me—shaping my heart and enriching my life.

About the Authors

Kerry Owen is an advocate, visionary, and mother of five whose commitment to tackling issues like poverty and food insecurity has inspired communities in New Zealand and the United States.

As the founder of Feed the Need in New Zealand, Kerry developed innovative programs to address food insecurity, including a free school lunch programme that gained national attention and paved the way for a government-funded school lunch programme. She has a knack for bringing large corporations and other nonprofits on board, creating dynamic collaborations that amplify the impact of these critical initiatives. Her dedication to being in the trenches and working directly with those she serves has garnered widespread support, establishing her as a respected influencer in the field of social impact.

In Utah, Kerry leads Reach Out Today, a nonprofit dedicated to empowering vulnerable children, youth, and refugees as they navigate life's critical transitions. Through Reach Out Today, she spearheaded a successful transitional housing project for youth aging out of foster care, providing stability and opportunities for those at risk of homelessness. Her unique perspective and fresh ideas have positioned her as a trusted voice in her field, leading her to share her insights through guest lectures and other platforms.

Awarded the Member of the New Zealand Order of Merit (MZNZ) by Queen Elizabeth II for her contributions to children's welfare, Kerry is passionate about the power of community to uplift those in need. She strives to balance her charity work with a deep-rooted commitment to family life, always keeping her loved ones at the core of her mission to create lasting change.

Lisa Knowlton is an avid reader who enjoys learning about cultural arts, history, and human relationships. She received a BA in Humanities with an emphasis in English from Brigham Young University. She especially enjoys British literature and the many movie adaptations of her favorites. She has enjoyed being part of the same book club for 26 years as its president.

Lisa has enjoyed teaching and directing sessions in the Especially for Youth and For the Strength of Youth programs with her husband, Ben, for twenty years. She has served on the board of Reach Out Today, a non-profit organization that addresses food insecurity and other needs in Utah. She is presently employed at BYU as a programme coordinator and event planner, working to foster a community of belonging among college students.

Lisa and her husband live in Springville, Utah, and have raised five sons. They are now enjoying empty nesting and grandparenthood. They plan to live life in crescendo as they look forward to new adventures.